Charlestown Blues

Acknowledgments

Grateful acknowledgment is given to the editors of the journals and anthologies in which many of these translations first appeared:

Agni (U.S.): "Blue Gold"; "The Veil of Ether" (online edition)

Barrow Street (U.S.): "Letter to the Unknown Woman across the Street, I"

Chelsea (U.S.): "Letter to Félicien Rops"; "The Raising of Icarus: Prologue"; "Yannis Ritsos"; "Max Jacob"; "In February"

Field (U.S.): "O Caravels"; "The Chair-Caner"

The Kenyon Review (U.S.): "To Cavafy"; "The Forgotten Traveler"

Kestrel (U.S.): "The Ascent of the Sonnet"

Literary Imagination (U.S.): "The Construction-Site of the Elegy"

The Massachusetts Review (U.S.): *From* "The Raising of Icarus": "The Shepherd Reproached"; "The Shepherd Answers"

Modern Poetry in Translation (U.K.): "The Construction-Site of the Elegy"

The New England Review (U.S.): "Envoi to The Raising of Icarus"

New Letters (U.S.): "Christmas Rimbe"; "Mont-Olympe"; "False Lélian"; "Ducal Ducasse"; "Passing on the Torch"; "Music in the Square"

The Paris Review (U.S.): "Boarding the Streetcar"

Poetry (U.S.): "Cuckoo's Bread"

Poetry International (U.S.): "Four Seasons for Jude Stéfan"

Poetry London (U.K.): "Letter to the Unknown Woman across the Street, II"; "Flesh-back"; "Passing on the Torch"; "Farewell, Châteaux"; "O Caravels"

PN Review (U.K.): "Waiting"; "Four Seasons for Jude Stéfan"; "Letter to my Postman"; "Cuckoo's Bread"

River Styx (U.S.): "Waiting"

TriQuarterly (U.S.): "In Memory of W. H. Auden"; "Poet in Gröningen"

Washington Square (U.S.): "Letter to my Postman"

The Faber Anthology of 20th Century French Poems, Stephen Romer, Ed. (U.K.): "Christmas Rimbe"; "False Lélian"; "Rondissimo"; "Letter to the Unknown Woman across the Street, I"; "III"; "Music in the Square"

The Yale Anthology of 20th Century French Poetry, Mary Ann Caws, Ed. (U.S.): "Max Jacob"; "Rondissimo"

Preface

Guy Goffette is one of the most unabashedly lyrical contemporary French poets, at a time when, for English language readers at least, contemporary French poetry is characterized, or caricatured, as abstract, more concerned with concepts than with human experience (including history) and feeling: resolutely "difficult." Here is a poet whose work is diffused with humor, longing, tenderness, nostalgia, and occasional cruelty, who does not hestitate to hint, at least, at narrative. He makes use of the quirks of language (follow the sentences and transformations meandering within his parentheses if you can) to mirror the quirks of thought; his deployment of myth is never far from concrete and earthy evocations of childhood, of emotional loss, or physical passion.

Guy Goffette was born in Jamoigne, in the Lorraine region, but on the Belgian side of the border, in 1947. This bit of geography has been French and Belgian at different times in its history, and the shifting and permeability of borders has always been primary among the poet's subjects. He lived in northern France for many years, and worked as a bookseller and as a schoolteacher. His austere and prematurely ruptured childhood is eloquently invoked in a book of literary memoir, *Partance et autres lieux*, published in 2000, which also sets forth some keys to his work:

> *Once, I dreamed of leaving for the sake of leaving and I always returned. Now I leave without budging, and there is no coming back. "You never leave" wrote Rimbaud, which could also be understood as: one never stops leaving, and the real journeys aren't the ones you'd think. That nonexistent sea beyond the poplars is more real to me than the sea, and farther away than all the Abyssinias. It's enough to let myself go.*

(Rimbaud's "On ne part pas" occurs more than once as a reference or an epigraph in Guy Goffette's writings.)

Nonetheless, he has traveled, both near—back and forth between Belgium and France, all through France, and in the Netherlands—and far, to Greece, to Eastern Europe, to pre-Katrina Louisiana, on the trail of the blues. Like his friend and early mentor, the poet Jacques Réda, he is a jazz enthusiast. He lives now in central Paris, where he works as an editor at Gallimard, and is closely but informally allied with poet-friends of his generation like Hédi Kaddour and Paul de Roux.

Goffette's voice dialogues with these and lively others in the land-scape of modern and contemporary French poetry (although even cultivated French readers who buy the new Quignard, even the new Cixous, and can catch a quote from Ronsard or Baudelaire, will all too often say that they know nothing of contemporary poetry, and don't like what they know). The Oulipian Jacques Roubaud, who is nonetheless a melancholy chronicler of the changing cityscape and an unforgettable elegist; the *piéton de Paris* in rhymed verse and in prose, Jacques Réda; Hédi Kaddour, whose sonnet-like aperçus of contem-porary life imply historical narrative behind them; the also-Belgian William Cliff, one of the few European Francophone *poets* since Genet to write openly—in rhymed stanzas and sonnets—about gay sexuality; the much younger Valérie Rouzeau, who marries a slangy demotic diction to received or metered forms, are a few of these. Ver-laine, the critic Jacques Borel reminds us, was the poet whom Rilke's Malte Laurids Brigge evoked as his exemplar of the art—and since Borel wrote this in an essay about Goffette, we are, and not errone-ously, invited to think of Rilke, Verlaine, and Goffette triangulated, and consider what the contemporary poet has drawn from these two past poles. If Goffette's lyrics sometimes partake of a density and sim-plicity of emotional thrust combined with prosodic *legerdemain* that is reminiscent of Verlaine, his attention to the tactile world, to objects as well as landscape, almost as much sculptorly as painterly, connects him with that master of the quotidian still-life (and of transcendence through the quotidian), Jean Follain, whose work (except for one book of urban prose sketches) also returns almost obsessively to rural landscapes of childhood and youth.

The publication of Goffette's *Éloge pour une cuisine de province* in 1988 brought the poet—already the author of several small-press collections—to the attention of a literary readership accustomed to ignoring poetry. The book's central paradox: the longing of one who muses men were not made, after all, to live in houses, but to pause in trees like migratory birds, while chronicling the palimpsests of life within the house's walls, within its kitchened heart; its evocation of the dreams and daring born in northern "villages of dark, cold schist" where a child of ten with "eternity under his cap" waits impatiently to grow up, gave readers some of the satisfactions and recognition they had come to expect only from fiction, while reminding them subtly of poetry's too-long ignored connection with song. Goffette's three subsequent books of poems, from which this present collection is taken, published between 1991 and 2001, explore the themes he set for himself (which seemed, like Proust's opening volume, to contain the possibility of a lifetime's elaborations) while deploying more knowingly, with more of a virtuoso's hand, the possibilities of poetic form and shape (received form, invented form, metrics used in homage, slant and internal rhyme), as the speaker's journey takes him well beyond the poplars at road's edge.

But where did his imagination's journey take him, after all? Paris is more central to French writing, poetry and prose, than any city in the United States has been to American literature. Among contemporary poets for whom landscape, narration, and context are significant, the city *intra muros* figures largely in the work of Raymond Queneau, Michel Deguy, Marie-Claire Bancquart, Franck Venaille, Hédi Kaddour, Jacques Roubaud, and Jacques Réda, to name a few. But Goffette, thoroughly contemporary, aligned to several of these poets in style, and aspiring to the same models (which include Pavese, Hölderlin, Cavafy, Borges, Auden) finds the sources of his work almost entirely in the provinces, not so much in a richness of local tradition (barely mentioned) as in a sense of being in a place from which his speaker is perpetually ready to depart. Paris—as a destination or a setting—is barely present. Even the streetcar in the urban/ekphrastic poem from a Lartigue photograph is, in fact, making its way down a New York avenue, not a Hausmannian boulevard. The closest the poems in this collection come to Paris is the evocation of the working-class and immigrant *banlieues* in the sequence "Cuckoo's Bread," where the Touareg child and the Kabyle merchant in the poem's present, when juxtaposed with the remembered father's vulnerable work-hardened hands, seem to promise to and share with the speaker a depth of (different) memory and a larger horizon.

One does not "leave" a place behind (physically or in spirit) without, often enough, leaving people, or a particular person. The theme of love and rupture, or separation, of desire and detumescence in more than its merely physical aspect, is a constant presence in Goffette's poems. Perhaps its most striking occurrence in this collection is the sequence "Waiting" (*L'attente*) in which the woman perpetually waiting for her peripatetic lover is given a voice, wounded, earthy, and powerful—in counterpart nonetheless to the disabused libertine voice (in Verlaine's and Rimbaud's shadow) of the solitary speaker in the "Charlestown Blues" sequence. The evocation of the erotic in Goffette's work is both discreet and powerful, working through indirection (the view of the ceiling after coitus, the repeated motif of a glimpsed stocking, more evocative than nudity), acknowledging the point of view of the male who sees both promise/redemption and the chill mortal shadow in the act of love and its release, both fantasies less than inclusive of a partner's point of view. (Another poem, a "true" sonnet not translated here, based on a painting by a contemporary artist, Catherine Lopès-Curval, is in the voice of an abandoned lover who transforms herself into a harpy-like bird of prey and flies off having had her revenge, still wearing lacework stockings.)

Goffette makes frequent homage to his sources, however oblique, in an ongoing series of *"Dilectures"*—doubled readings of predilection and delectation. *Dilection* is a literary French word for "cherishing," or the love of God for the created world—but there is an undercurrent of misreading, "unreading," "disreading" in the neologism as well. These poems are deft verse portraits of writers as diverse as Auden, Ritsos, Borges, Max Jacob, Valéry Larbaud, Pound, Pavese, Rimbaud, and, of course, Verlaine, to whom Goffette also devoted an innovative prose book, neither biography nor criticism but a poet's re-imagination of another poet's life and mind. Goffette claims Verlaine, product of a similar geography, as one of his literary godfathers without any compunction, with no scorn, quite the contrary, for the musicality, eroticism, and nostalgia associated with Verlaine's poetry.

He has written a similar volume on Bonnard, and some of his poetic homages are to visual artists as well—in this collection, the Symbolist artist Félicien Rops and the photographer Jean-Henri Lartigue;

in *Un Manteau de Fortune*, to Catherine Lopès-Curval, above. Auden, that least French of poets and critics, has fascinated Guy Goffette for years, and a recent book, *L'Oeil de la baleine*, addresses him in a equally idiosyncratic prose encounter. The long sequence called "The Raising of Icarus" refers indirectly at once to Auden's poem "Musée des Beaux-Arts" and to the Brueghel painting which inspired it.

Despite these homages and acknowledgements of origins, Goffette's is not a "literary," referential poetry, if that means a poetry which requires a gloss or footnotes to be understood; nor is it self-referential as American autobiographical poetry might be taken to be (or the fashionable French "auto-fiction"). I believe that Guy Goffette's poetry can be enjoyed even by a reader whose ear does not vibrate to the often-present echoes; and the writers or painters of his homages come alive as independent portrait subjects. Whatever echoes he calls forth, Goffette is a poet who makes use (as Paul Claudel, himself the subject of a lengthy "dilecture," proposed in his own *ars poetica*) of quotidian words, everyday expressions, and makes them new (as Ezra Pound, elsewhere "disread," directed), re-invests them with humor, connotation, and emotion, and with a tragicomic festivity. He is also a poet whose work, in subtext, dialogues with the past of French poetry itself, though this dialogue is an undercurrent, never diverting the poem from its primary direction. The bold and witty "Charlestown Blues," for example, written during a residence in Rimbaud's Charleville, makes use of the decasyllabic dixain, which a French reader would associate not with the Verlaine/Rimbaud duo/duet/duel but with Maurice Scève's mysterious "Délie," published in Lyon in 1544.

As part of this dialogue, Guy Goffette's ludic tug-of-war with the sonnet, which is evident in his three most recent books, is one attraction, for me, as a poet, to his work. Like Goffette, I myself have often handled (or mauled), de- and reconstructed the form. Goffette has written—and continues occasionally to write—wry, contemporary rhymed sonnets in alexandrines. But a thirteen-line poem, as part of a sequence or standing on its own, made up of three usually unrhymed quatrains and a last line which sometimes, though not always, mounts to the classic twelve syllables, has become Goffette's "signature" strophe since his 1991 collection, *La vie promise*; he has continued to use it in his two subsequent books. A poet whose references and homages attest to a mastery of received forms, he cautions that, in most of his own writing, he "brushes up against classical versification in passing," preferring a studied "limping" to syllabic perfection. He makes playful reference to his own chosen form in the sequence "The Ascent of the Sonnet"—as he does to simile and its inevitability, even to the caesura (which has a more significant place in the alexandrine than it does in English iambic pentameter, precisely because the pentameter is accentual, and the alexandrine syllabic). It shouldn't be necessary to add, though, that "the sonnet" in this sequence is only "the subject" in that Goffette uses it to demonstrate what, in his eyes, any poem exists to accomplish: to build a ladder on which the mind can mount to effect a rescue—however temporary, however figurative—from the scaffold of mortality.

Though Guy Goffette is not an Anglicist, he has made known his admiration for English language poetry, for its specificity and concreteness; his admiration for Philip Larkin and for Robert Frost, as well as for Auden: an unlikely trio who share, however, metrical perfect pitch, a disabused vision of humanity, and a sense nonetheless of human depth beneath apparent drabness. Given Goffette's fondness for homages, it is interesting for an American reader (such as myself) to consider in which other English language poets' work, whether or not known to Guy Goffette, there can be found *correspondances* in the Baudelairean sense, and resonances with the poems in this book. The first such poet to come to my mind is James Wright. Both poets (to my mind) share a post-Romantic rather than a post-Modernist sensibility. Their sojourns in cities are equally uneasy; the perpetual appeal of an "elsewhere" is ubiquitous, as are the echoes of a dystopic childhood and a certain solitary's pessimism about human nature. Both also draw frequently on an early mastery of classical forms, which remain a referent, often an echo, even in an open-form poem. Both of their poetic personae view the act of love and the emotions which lead to it and which it engenders (it doesn't engender anything else in the poems) as inspiration/salvation and as a reminder of impermanence and mortality. But another reference point for an Anglophone might well be the poetry of Seamus Heaney. Among the things Goffette and Heaney share is a solidity of place, and of objects, with an emphasis on the perceived material thing, its implications suggested. For both poets, the return to a Bronze Age (rather than a Golden Age) of childhood is recurrent, called up by *things* and by sensations; both, too, carry on an ongoing dialogue with the sonnet form, sometimes modifying and inflecting it at will. The poem-homages or *dilectures* are also a point in common, prevalent all through both of their work: Cavafy, Auden, and Pavese (at least) have been the subjects of poems by both Goffette and Heaney. The métro sequence in Goffette's "Raising of Icarus" finds an uncanny echo in Heaney's most recent book, where, in a sonnet sequence, a similarly unsettled traveler descends into a Dantesque London Underground.

After a period in which much highly acclaimed French poetry eschewed the concrete, the lyrical, the narrative, and the quotidian, Guy Goffete's poems have found an enthusiastic readership in the last fifteen years. He received the Grand prix de poésie of the Société des gens de lettres in 1999 for the entirety of his work, and, in 2001, the Grand prix de poésie de l'Académie française for *Un manteau de fortune*. His 1988 collection *Éloge pour une cuisine de province* along with *La vie promise* were reissued in Gallimard's popular pocket-format Poésie series in 2000. At once erotic and lyrical, urbane and unabashedly pastoral, of its time and in constant colloquy with a plethora of traditions, his work ought to help widen the dialogue between Anglophone and Francophone poetry beyond the most resolutely "experimental" schools. But Goffette's poetry is not here to be exemplary, and is singularly unfit for a missionary position: it is here as a source of musical pleasure, of memory-seasoned food for thought, as one more irresistible "invitation to the voyage."

Marilyn Hacker
Paris, October 2006

Blues à Charlestown: Vieux Dixains Charlestown Blues

Rimbe de Noël
à William Cliff

On a vendu le vieux piano d'herbes
aux neiges de l'Ardenne. Adieux les muses
vertes du *Mont-Olympe*, nous n'irons
plus surprendre les deux amants: l'hiver
les a figés dans la Meuse de glace;
et Rimbe, s'il reparaît, c'est en croûte
dans la vitrine des charcuteries
où trône une tête de veau (elle a
deux trous rouges qui clignotent pour rien:
Charleville a ses illuminations).

Mont-Olympe

C'est un petit Vésuve tout vert et
bien éteint qui domine le quai, l'eau
ballante où l'éphèbe rageur boutait
le feu de Dieu aux voyelles mourantes
des roseaux. On y monte le dimanche
à pied, en passant devant le moulin
et sur le fleuve aux bateaux impassibles,
où des demoiselles à petits culs roses,
qui craignent les Indiens, s'exposent nues
aux flèches caniculaires, et rôtissent.

Christmas Rimbe
to William Cliff

They've sold the old piano made of grass
to the Ardennes' snow. Farewell green muses
of Mont-Olympe, never again will we
flush out that pair of lovers: winter's fixed
them forever in the Meuse of ice;
and Rimbe, if he came back, he would be swathed
in piecrust in the delicatessen
window, where a calf-head's enthroned (it has
two red holes which blink and blink for nothing:
Charleville has its own illuminations).

Mont-Olympe

A miniature Vesuvius, all green,
but dormant, surmounts the dock, the slack
water, where the raging ephebe drove out
God's' fire into the dying vowels
of the reeds. People go up on Sunday
afternoon strolls, pass the mill, walk along
the river with its unflappable boats
where girls with bare pink buttocks, though afraid
of Redskins, still expose their nudity
to the arrows of the dog-days, and roast.

Faux Lélian
pour Franz Bartelt

Verlaine au fond de *L'Idéal Bar*, s'il
écœure tant la jeune rousse assise
sous les lustres de Murano, les têtes
de bois sculptées dans la frise ou mûrissent
pour des prunes les grappes du Seigneur,
c'est qu'il faut plus qu'une barbe pisseuse,
un air de ressemblance et dégoiser
sa vie sur neuf pieds « à la manière de »
pour mériter de boire tout son saoul
aux lèvres des Carolopolitaines.

Rondissimo
à Jacques Réda

S'il tangue un peu par grands vents, ce deuxième
que j'habite rue de Mantoue, ce n'est
pas qu'il soit vieux ni à portée de mer,
mais d'être à l'enseigne de *Rebecca*,
où, comme proue et poupe d'un bateau
callipyge, les dames bien en chair
balancent—et leurs rires troublent l'âme
du solitaire ensablé dans ses mots,
à deux pas du petit Harrar, au bout
de cette rue qui monte, où Rimbaud dort.

False Lélian
for Franz Bartelt

Verlaine ensconced in the Ideal Bar,
if he disgusts the young redhead seated
under Murano chandeliers and wood
heads sculpted on the molding where the Lord's
grape-clusters ripen for beans, it's because
it takes more than a piss-yellow beard, a
familiar air, a tendency to spout
one's life out in nine beats "in the style of"
to merit drinking to your fill from the
lips of the Carolopolitan girls.

Rondissimo
to Jacques Réda

If it sways in the wind, this second floor
where I'm living in the rue de Mantoue,
it's not because it's old or near the sea,
but above the awning of "Rebecca,"
where, prow and poop of a callipygous
boat, full-figured ladies float in and out
and their laughter troubles the hermit soul
silted in his own words, two steps away
from the little Harrar at the summit
of this steep-mounting street, where Rimbaud sleeps.

Lettre à l'inconnue d'en face, 1

Rideaux, tentures, voilages, non rien,
Madame, pour dérober à votre œil
de cyclope dans l'ombre qui m'épie
ce long corps nu de faux gisant recru
d'intempérances, et qui se pâme aussi
devant votre balcon où sèche toute
une lingerie de nonne aux abois—
fleurs vénéneuses pour le solitaire
que la mort affole dresse démoelle
dans la nuit, rivé à vos blanches cuisses.

Ducasse ducale
pour André Velter

Ô jours de pluie et de maigre pitance,
cantine ouverte aux poètes qui pleurent
la mer allée sur la triste *éternit*
et sur l'ardoise, suffit. Laissez-moi
partir un peu vers des soleils plus ivres
que cet Orient de bimbeloterie
sous la bâche bleue du marché, laissez-
moi mordre dans l'azur et, comme l'ange
aux yeux de barbarie, boire à mon tour
l'alcool vertigineux des Hespérides.

Letter to the Unknown Woman across the Street, 1

Curtains, blinds, draperies, shades, no, nothing
Madame, to conceal from your Cyclops' eye
in the shadows from which it spies on me
this long pale body, false corpse tired out
with debauchery, which is swooning too
before your balcony, with your drying
stockings and scanties of a nun at bay—
poisonous flowers for a lonely man
whom death panics, draws erect, demarrows
in the night, riveted to your white thighs.

Ducal Ducasse
for André Velter

Oh days of rain and meager sustenance,
mess-hall open to poets weeping for
the sea gone off over sad *éternit*
and slate roofs alike, enough! Let me go
away a while in search of suns more drunk
than this makeshift Orient beneath the
market-stalls' blue awnings, let me bite in-
to the azure, and, like the angel with
savage eyes, let me have my turn to drink
the heady wine of the Hesperides.

Lettre à l'inconnue d'en face, 2

Si peu de lumière sur ma table, si
peu que les mots comme fleurs rabougrissent
—et ma chair, si vous n'y portez remède
par saoules salives, si votre ventre
fougueusement ne l'enroule, ma chair
vive et veuve livrée nue chaque nuit
à votre délectation s'en ira
elle aussi pétale à pétale avant
que nous n'ayons trouvé, belle inconnue,
cette bête qui voyage beaucoup.

Flache back

L'espoir couleur de paille luit parfois
au fond des cafés bleus parce qu'un brin
de soleil à l'or des chopes s'allume,
et chacun se tourne comme une fleur
avide vers la *flache* de ciel chu
sur l'asphalte, ô vieux miroir de benzine
où le galopin hirsute qu'on fut
dans une autre vie reviendra taper
de son pied vengeur merde merde et merde
à l'atone éternité des provinces.

Letter to the Unknown Woman across the Street, 2

So little light on my work-table, so
little that my words shrivel like flowers
—as will my flesh, if you bring no relief
in salacious saliva, if your thighs
do not ardently envelop it, my
flesh, alive, unloved, delivered nightly
for your delectation, will disappear
also, petal by petal, before we
have ever found, oh beautiful stranger,
that creature who's so often on the move.

Flesh-back

A straw-colored hope sometimes glimmers in
the back-rooms of cafés, when one sun-ray's
enough to light up the gold in the beer
and everyone there turns like an avid
flower toward the flesh-flash of sky fallen
on asphalt, oh old mirror of benzine
where the long-haired urchin you once were in
another life will come back to stamp with
his vengeful foot shit shit and again shit
at unstressed provincial eternity.

Lettre à l'inconnue d'en face, 3

Reconnaissez Madame que mourir
hors du *dérèglement de tous les sens*
est triste et sans aucun profit (présent
gâché que la vertu, la nuit vient vite
et la plus belle rose est du fumier).
Ouvrez vos ombres votre giron vos
lèvres: le clou du spectacle est en bas
dans la rue où, preste comme une main
sous les robes, le vent réveille les
beaux orages qui nous étaient promis.

Portrait de R. en retour de bâton
pour Alain Borer

Ô vent d'hiver chassant la pluie comme
un jars les poules sur le pavé,
vent à renverser le Commandeur
sur son socle de marbre, viens et
change la nuit en désert, ce pas
de rôdeur en une jambe unique
et roide frappant sous les arcades
J A R comme affront aux marchands
du temple et salut aux chiens aux fous
aux simples qui dorment avec les lys.

Letter to the Unknown Woman across the Street, 3

Admit, Madame, that to die not having
known *the derangement of all the senses*
is sad and useless (virtue is only
the present spoiled, night falls fast, and the most
beautiful rose is dung on the dung-heap).
Open up your shadows, your lap, your lips:
the pinnacle of the play is outside
down on the street where, nimble as a hand
under a dress, the wind awakens the
beautiful storms which were promised to us.

Passing on the Torch
for Alain Borer

O winter wind, driving the rain along
the pavement like a gander chasing hens,
wind which could knock the Commander off his
marble pedestal, come and
change this night into a desert, this
prowler's pace into a single stiff
leg stamping beneath the archways
J A R confronting the merchants in
the temple and hail to the dogs the mad
the simple who sleep among the lilies.

Square à musique
à Jude Stéfan

Plus d'*absomphe* au Café de l'Univers,
l'un a retrouvé l'autre sous la glaise
et se fiche de tout: la pluie condamne
au muscadet la clique infortunée
comme un cheval piaffant au comptoir
tandis que sur les *mesquines pelouses*,
une gamine un peu rosse et qui sait
sauter sur les couacs, tire la langue
à la statue du poète fleuri
et montre sa culotte en criant tintin.

Adieu châteaux

Ah partir (tout de suite ces hauts cris
de concierge. *On ne part pas*, trancha R.
en tordant le cou à l'azur qui met
toujours trop de miel sur la queue des vers)
comme si la route allait toute seule
sans vertige ni doutes—une colline,
soudain et la quille éclate, et la soif
revient d'almes caresses au val moussu.
Partir, ô gangrène du fol amour:
la vie à cru sur le dos des saisons.

Music in the Square
to Jude Stéfan

At the Café de l'Univers, no more
absomphe. They've found each other under the
clay, and don't give a damn. The rain condemns
the unlucky brass band to muscadet
like a horse pawing the ground at the bar
while outside on the *penny-pinching lawns*
a cheerful, rather nasty little girl
sticks out her tongue at the poet's statue
and then, a beat ahead of their wrong notes
flashes her underpants, shouting Ta-Dum!

Farewell, Châteaux

To leave (all at once, those shrill concierge's
cries. *You never leave*, snapped R, as he wrung
the neck of the azure, which always puts
too much honey on the tails of verse-worms)
as if the road unrolled itself alone
without doubts or dizziness—a sudden
hill, and the keel explodes, a thirst comes back
to be safely stroked in mossy valleys.
To leave, gangrene of crazy love, to live
one's life raw on the back of the seasons.

Février '98

Avec six mois de retard sur les oies
sauvages, cent vingt-neuf ans après l'as
des fugueurs ardennais et son *merdre* à
la poisseuse poésie, j'ai quitté
Charleville et l'inconnue d'en face
dont les dentelles festonnées de givre
battaient avec mon cœur contre la vitre.
J'ai fait un signe à la Meuse baignant
dans sa luxure, verte, et dit Allons,
mais sur deux jambes, au diable le génie.

February '98

Six months later than the wild geese and a
hundred-twenty-nine years after the ace
of fugitives from the Ardennes and his
Fuck off! to puttering poetry, I've left
Charleville and the stranger across the street
whose lacy underwear festooned with frost
beat with my heart against the window-pane.
I waved good-bye to the Meuse as she bathed
in her green lechery, and said Let's go!
but on two feet, the devil take genius.

La Montée au Sonnet The Ascent of the Sonnet

Ô Caravelles

On ne part pas. RIMBAUD

I

Enfant, je savais comme partir est doux
pour n'avoir jamais quitté la barque
des collines, fendu l'autre horizon
que la pluie quand elle ferme le matin,

et q'il me fallait à tout prix trouver
la bonne lumière pour poser les mers
à leur place sur la carte et ne pas
déborder. J'avais dix ans et

plus de voyages dans mes poches
que les grands navigateurs, et si
je consentais à échanger la Sierra

Leone contre la Yakoutie, c'est que
vraiment la dentelle de neige
autour du timbre était la plus forte.

II

pour Paul de Roux

Vieux et perdu comme un cheval
au bord du clos de l'équarrissage,
et mort d'avance à toute idée de retour
dans l'herbe tendrement verte

O Caravels

You never leave. RIMBAUD

I

A child, I knew how sweet departure was
from having never left the skiff
of hills, split open any horizon
but the rain's when it closed off the morning

and that I'd have to find at any cost
the right light so that I could fix the seas
in their places on the map and not
overflow the lines. I was ten and

had more voyages in my pockets
than the great explorers, and if
I agreed to trade Sierra

Leone for Yakoutia, it's really
because the snowy frame of lace
around the stamp was sturdier.

II

for Paul de Roux

Old and lost like a horse
outside the slaughter-house yard
already dead to any possible return
to the tenderly green grass

du passé, je lécherai peut-être aussi
le salpêtre des murs. Le ciel fasse
qu ce soit comme ce frère à Turin
qui lécha le visage de Nietzsche

où tout—grandeur, effroi, savoir,
avait sombré, ne laissant
au milieu des larmes et parmi les rieurs
qu'un homme comme une route

quand elle ouvre la mer.

of the past, perhaps I'd also lick
saltpeter from the walls. Let Heaven arrange
for it to be like the brother in Turin
who licked Nietzsche's face

where everything—grandeur, terror, knowledge—
had foundered, leaving nothing
in the midst of tears and among the mockers
but a man like a road

when it cleaves the sea.

L'Attente

Si tu viens pour rester, dit-elle, ne parle pas.
Il suffit de la pluie et du vent sur les tuiles,
il suffit du silence que les meubles entassent
comme poussière depuis des siècles sans toi.

Ne parle pas encore. Écoute ce qui fut
lame dans ma chair: chaque pas, un rire au loin,
l'aboiement du cabot, la portière qui claque
et ce train qui n'en finit pas de passer

sur mes os. Reste sans paroles: il n'y a rien
à dire. Laisse la pluie redevenir la pluie
et le vent cette marée sous les tuiles, laisse

le chien crier son nom dans la nuit, la portière
claquer, s'en aller l'inconnu en ce lieu nul
où je mourais. Reste si tu viens pour rester.

Je sais, criait-elle, je sais: les téléphones
n'existent pas, c'est partout la fin du monde,
les gens s'écrasent sur les trottoirs,
on meurt debout, de dos, de face,

sans prévenir. Il n'y a plus que les chats
pour savoir décliner le mot amour
au bord du précipice, et tant pis pour ceux
qui dorment en paix, tant pis

Waiting

I

If you've come to stay, she says, don't speak.
The rain and the wind on the roof-tiles are enough
and the silence piled up on the furniture
like dust for centuries without you.

Don't speak yet. Listen to what was
the knife in my flesh: each step, a far-off laugh,
some mongrel barking, the car door slamming
and that train which continues to pass and pass

over my bones. Keep still: there's nothing to say.
Let the rain turn into rain again
and the wind be that tide beneath the roof-tiles, let

the cur cry his name into the night, the car door
slam, the stranger leave, in this null place
where I was dying. Stay if you've come to stay.

II

I know, she would cry out, I know: telephones
don't exist, it's the end of the world everywhere,
people are flattened on the sidewalk,
they're dying on their feet, behind you, in front of you

with no warning. There's no one but cats left
capable of declining the noun love
at the edge of the cliff, and too bad for those
who rest in peace, a pity

pour la plaine inconsolable: toujours du blé,
toujours du bleu et pas le plus petit grain
de montagne à l'horizon, le moindre

écho de toi dans ce désert immense,
pas la plus légère secousse au bout du fil
comme une voix pour endormir la nuit.

III

Détrompe-toi, dit-elle encore, il n'y a pas
que mes lèvres, mes seins, pas que mon ventre
à t'attendre, à surseoir d'un jour, d'une heure même,
le jugement du vide qui m'écrase

comme un insecte sur la vitre, non. Il y a loin
de la mer à cette plage où tes vagues,
l'une après l'autre, viennent accoucher du vent.
Il y a, dit-elle, il y a

ce qui est sans visage, sans voix: un champ de neige
derrière la haie—l'hiver y dure depuis si longtemps
que tes soleils, tes glorieux soleils

de fin de semaine, s'ils le frôlent jamais,
y fondent aussitôt—et je reste à t'attendre,
seule et glacée, sous tes caresses.

for the inconsolable plain: always that wheat,
always that blue, and not the slightest grain
of mountain on the horizon, not the least

echo of you in this enormous desert,
not the briefest tremor on the line
like a voice to put the night to sleep.

III

Don't fool yourself, she said again, it isn't only
my mouth, my breasts, not only my womb
that waits for you, to postpone for a day, an hour
the judgment of this absence crushing me

like an insect on the pane, no. There is, far
from the sea, with that beach where your waves
come, one after another, to give birth to wind.
There is, she says, there is

something faceless, voiceless: a field of snow
behind the hedge—winter has lasted there so long
that your suns, your glorious weekend

suns, were they ever to brush across it,
would melt instantly—and I'd be waiting
for you, alone and frozen beneath your touch.

IV

C'est dans une île qu'il aurait fallu,
disait-elle souvent, une île un peu égarée
mais quand même tenant tête au vent,
une avec des arbres verts et nombreux,

de quoi se perdre, s'oublier, reprendre un visage
qui ne ressemble qu'à soi, où dure l'étonnement
d'être, et savoir si le cœur est encore
à sa place, maître à bord du vieux navire.

Oui, c'est dans une île, dans une île
qu'il aurait fallu ouvrir l'un après l'autre,
peu à peu, notre unique trésor, et non

l'étaler comme ici, parmi les rognures du temps,
tout jouer d'un coup de dés sur le tapis
et puis demander au plafond l'heure du train.

IV

It should have been on some island
she'd say often, an island that had lost its way
but still held its own against the wind,
one with numerous green trees

where one could lose oneself, forget oneself, get back
that face that looks only like itself, where the surprise
of being lasts, could know if the heart is still
in place, captain of the old ship.

Yes, it's on an island, on an island
where, taking turns, we should have opened,
layer by layer, our only treasure, not

laid it out as we do here, amidst time's peelings,
bet everything on dice tossed on the carpet
and then asked the ceiling when the next train leaves.

Parenthèse noir

I

Le corps de l'homme en proie
à l'errance s'habitue vite
au visage nombreux de la mort:
fatigue, dégoût, ruine de tous

projets, ces promesses pas à pas
qui reculent, s'enfoncent dans l'hier
et la nuit. Sur quoi vient la rouille
du moindre geste. On dirait

qu'elle se pose comme une feuille
quand le sang ne veut plus courir,
à bout de tant de regrets, remords,
soupirs, ce qu'on porte malgré soi:

l'encombrant bouclier des vaincus.

II

On s'habitue vite et c'est ce qui
nous sauve, paraît-il. Encore petit
et peu sûr au dedans, et triste déjà
à cause d'un lapin mort de froid

dans sa cage, d'une fleur piétinée, bref,
c'était pire encore de les entendre
s'exclamer: regarde comme il s'est
endurci, tant sont aveugles ceux

Dark Parenthesis

I

A man's body subject to
vagrancies quickly gets used
to the multiple faces of death:
fatigue, disgust, dilapidation

of every project, promises that retreat
step by step, sink into yesterday
and darkness. And on them the rust
of the least gesture. You could say

that it settles like a leaf
when your blood no longer wants to flow
after so much regret, remorse,
sighs, what you bear despite yourself:

the cumbersome shield of the vanquished.

II

We get used to it fast and that's
what saves us, it seems. Still small
and inwardly unsure, and sad already
because of a rabbit dead of cold

in its cage, a trampled flower, in short
it was still worse to hear them
exclaim: look how tough
he's gotten, they are so blind

qui voient bien l'écorce aux prises
avec la pluie, la grêle, mais jamais
la grimace de l'aubier ou du surgeon
malmené (votre enfant, grand dieu!

si plein de larmes et d'effroi).

III

Bien sûr, elles finissent par sécher,
les larmes, dans le recès des pères
et mères, le devoir, l'exemple et la
virilité, comme le foutre plus tard

sur la beauté défaite, l'amour trahi,
avec la honte d'être nu, dépossédé
du vertige de l'arbre sur le ciel
quand l'éternité tendait son royaume

jusque dans nos bras d'enfant. Bien sûr,
elles sèchent (nous sommes devenus
des hommes, prêts à battre les monts
à la course), mais comme nos vies

se lézardent vite, qui ne débordent plus.

they who can see the bark grappling
the rain, the hail, but never
the sapwood's grimace or the
mangled taproot's (your child, good god!

brimming over with tears and terror).

III

Of course, in the end they dry up,
those tears, in the retreat of fathers
and mothers, in duty, in good examples, and
virility, like jism later

on the undone beauty, love betrayed
in the shame of being naked, dispossessed
of the tree's vertigo against the sky
when eternity held out its kingdom

to our childish arms. Of course
they dry up (we've become
men, ready to beat mountains
in the race), but, like our lives,

crack quickly, no longer overflow.

La Montée au sonnet
(Pour un art poétique)

MUSES

Seins de glace ou d'enfer, orage
en plaine et la mer entre les collines
agenouillant sans mot dire celui
qui n'avait soif que de lui-même.

Le tant présent à ses mots, le voici
sans paroles jeté hors du poème,
chair à nouveau et feu et eau,
porte battue battant le cœur

comme une grange dans l'été paille et poutre
avec la mort petite mais sourde
qui s'impatiente, voudrait parler,

parle, de plus en plus haut,
jusqu'à ne plus entendre qu'elle,
dans leur bouche, qui muse.

I

Treize encore et non douze ou quatorze,
malgré qu'on en ait, et comme pour ménager
un peu l'animal dans la montée au sonnet
et retarder la chute inévitable.

Si la voix tombe avant la fin du morceau,
c'est sans doute faute de vouloir une musique
autre que le silence élargissant le souffle
au-delà de soi-même.

The Ascent of the Sonnet
(Toward an Ars Poetica)

MUSES

Breasts of ice or devilish ones, storm
on the plain and the sea between the hills
bringing him wordless to his knees who once
knew no thirst but a thirst for himself.

The one so present to his own words, here he is
speechless thrown out of the poem,
flesh once more and fire and water
beaten door banging against the heart

like a barn in summer, straw and beams
with death there tiny but deaf
who's getting restless, wants to speak,

speaks, louder and louder
till nothing else can be heard
in their musing mouths.

I

Thirteen again and not twelve or fourteen
though you'd wish it otherwise, and as if to spare
your mount a bit in the ascent of the sonnet
and delay the inevitable fall.

If the voice drops before the end of the piece
doubtless it's because no music's wanted
but the silence broadening your breath
beyond yourself.

Comme le jardin d'ombres dans le trille
inachevé du roitelet prend toute sa mesure,
le treizième apôtre seul à table, ignorant
le pendu, lève son verre

à l'espace innombrable des étoiles.

II

Et puis tous ces *comme*, ces *encore*,
ces grosses chevilles de caissière,
comme disait l'autre en proie à la grammaire
et qui théorisait sur les racines,

à deux mètres du parterre de pissenlits
—je l'entends encore, c'était comme,
enfin, bon—e là-dessus la poussière et la dalle,
son dernier ploc mouchant d'un coup

tous les oiseaux du voisinage. Au retour,
buter sur un caillou faisait monter les larmes
et l'on se retenait aux chevilles de la caissière
que tous ces *comme*, ces petits malappris

menaient danser pour nous, devant, avec la pluie.

III

Et la césure qui se plante là-dedans
comme un type en salopette au milieu du bal
des sirènes. Allons bon, revoilà la marine
—mais comment dire je t'aime

As the shadow garden in the unfinished
trill of the winter wren takes his whole measure,
the thirteenth apostle, alone at the table, ignoring
the hanged man, raises his glass

to the unmetered distance of the stars.

II

And then all those *likes* and *as's*, those *agains*,
those cashier's swollen ankles,
as that other one used to say, gripped by grammar
and theorizing about roots

two yards from a bed of dandelions
—I can still hear him, it was like,
well, then—and on top of it the dust, the flagstones,
his last gob extinguishing all

the birds in the neighborhood at once. On the way back
butting against a pebble made tears well up
and one held fast to the cashier's ankles
which all those *likes*, those little rapscallions

led in a dance for us, in front of, with the rain.

III

And the caesura which parks itself right in the middle
like a guy in overalls in a ballroom full
of mermaids. There we go, the sea again
—but how can I say I love you

sans trébucher dans ses lacets? Le clair de lune
à l'heure électronique n'étrangle plus
que le visage en larmes d'un basset,
contre l'arche du pont, qui s'oublie,

oublie sa faim et sa misère: au bout
de sa longe, là-haut, la muse s'impatiente
qui tire comme un poète à la ligne, tire,
tandis qu'avec la lune passe au fil des reflets

l'âme de l'homme qui aboie.

IV

De ces mots de rien, de peu, ces verbes
ramassés sur la route et traînés dans la pluie
comme les papiers gras de la fête, à l'aube,
dans l'herbe écrasée,

faire une échelle pour grimper jusqu'au pendu
qui se balance à la maîtresse poutre
du Temps, couper la corde et envelopper
ce corps sans visage

dans la langue des collines, le bleu
ramage des oiseaux, la musique des cuisines
après le dernier repas, quand tout s'est éteint
et que la lune seule

remplit l'assiette du voyageur oublié.

without stumbling into its snares? The moonlight
in this electronic age only chokes up
the tearful face of a basset hound
against the bridge's curve, who forgets himself

forgets his hunger and his wretchedness: at the end
of her tether up there, the muse gets restless
and tugs like a poet at the line, tugs
while, along with the moon down the reflecting stream

goes the soul of the barking man.

IV

From these empty, scanty words, these verbs
picked up on the road, dragged through the rain
like candy wrappers from a fair, at dawn,
in the crushed grass,

build a ladder to climb up to the hanged man
who swings from the retaining beam
of time, cut the cord, and enfold
that faceless body

in the language of hills, the blue
music of birds, the songs of kitchens
after the day's last meal, when the lights are out
and when only the moon

fills up the plate of the forgotten traveler.

Une Question de Bleu A Question of Blue

Lettre à mon facteur

I

Été comme hiver, la barrière est ouverte,
paisible au fond le chien qui aboie
contre l'horizon vide, bien avant
que je t'aperçoive, et il n'y a guère

plus de vingt pas de la route au seuil
de ma maison, ni ronces dans l'allée
ni femme dure et sombre, personne
pour sortir les verres à pied, voir

la chaleur déplier ton visage
comme une lettre et, comme le désert
se traverse, brûler cette distance
qu'une boîte rouge et vide

t'empêche de franchir.

2

Je te le demande au lever, devant le miroir
quand tout peut encore advenir: une piqûre
de guêpe, le renversement du tyran,
l'explosion grandiose du mur

que le voisin a élevé sous mes fenêtres.
Je te le demande encore quand le soleil
retire son échelle et que mon ombre se confond
avec l'ombre de la toise mitoyenne,

Letter to my Postman

In summer as in winter, the gate is open,
and peaceful at heart the dog who barks
at the empty horizon, long before
I spot you, and there are hardly

more than twenty paces from the road to the threshold
of my house, neither brambles along the pathway
nor dour and gloomy wife, no one
to take out the wineglasses, see

warmth unfold your face
like a letter, and, as the desert
is crossed, burn up that distance
which an empty red box

prevents you from crossing.

2

I ask you this upon rising, in front of the mirror
when anything still might happen: the sting
of a wasp, the overthrow of a tyrant,
the grandiose explosion of the wall

which my neighbor has erected beneath my windows.
I ask you this again when the sun
takes its ladder away and my shadow blends
into the shadow of the wall we share

le bras noir du tyran resté debout
avec le dard précis de la guêpe qui viendra
un jour, déguisée, mais si sûre
de m'abattre; je te le demande:

quoi de neuf, ici, pour nous deux?

Le Rempailleur

Ce que cela a coûté pour que plie le vieux paysan
qui refusait de céder la terre des aïeux
et pour l'ensablement du marais, et le pontage
et la réception des hauts dignitaires, il l'ignore,
le peintre du dimanche voué aux fleurs,
aux yeux de chats, à l'éclosion des jeunes filles
sur la dune imaginaire, tout comme l'ignorent
les dieux de ce palais qui fument et parlent d'art
avec des gestes de statues grecques. Il sait
seulement que pour peindre un passereau dans le ciel
suffit, un rayon de soleil sur la paille de sa chaise,
pourvu qu'au fond du silence un instant se desserre
la poigne d'ombre qui fait trembler les yeux.

into the black arm of the still-standing tyrant
with the accurate dart of the wasp which will come
one day, disguised, but so sure
of doing me in: I ask you this:

what's new, here, for the two of us?

The Chair-Caner

Whatever it cost to make the old peasant give in
who had refused to yield his ancestors' land,
cost to have the swamp sanded over, and the bridge built
and the reception for state dignitaries, he knows nothing of it
the Sunday painter devoted to flowers
to cats' eyes, to young girls' blossoming
on an imaginary dune, just as such things are not noticed
by the gods of this palace who smoke and talk of art
with the gestures of Greek statues. He only
knows that for painting, a sparrow in the sky
suffices, or a sun-ray on the straw of his chair
if in the depth of silence for an instant that shadow
loosens the grip that makes him drop his eyes.

En février

Lui aussi croyait en sa force de tigre
et que la jeunesse est immortelle.
Il savait par cœur le chemin et le goût
du lait dans le bol ébréché,

mais que le sang fût amer et froid le métal
dans la tiédeur de l'aube : non. Un frisson
a parcouru son poil ébouriffé, libérant
un brin d'herbe si vert que j'ai suivi

des yeux son preste envol, le temps
d'un souffle, juste ce qu'il faut à la mort
pour traverser une vie de chat et jeter,
dans un bol de lait sur,

une belle journée de soleil, à jamais ébréchée.

In February

He too believed in his tiger's strength
and that youth is immortal.
He knew the road by heart and the taste
of milk in the chipped bowl,

but that blood was bitter and metal cold
in dawn's mildness: no. A shiver
crossed his rumpled fur, freeing
a blade of grass so green that I followed

its swift flight with my eyes, for a breath's
instant, all that it took for death
to cross a cat's life and toss
into a bowl of sour milk,

a fine sunny day, now chipped for good.

Chantier de l'élégie

À tondre l'herbe d'octobre—la dernière
avant la horde rousse et la poigne d'hiver,

le désespoir (ou quoi d'autre si demain
n'existe pas?) vous prend à la gorge,

et c'est peu dire qu'on résiste aux larmes
en touillant dans la farine verte.

La machine à côté crachote vaillamment
comme intoxiquée elle aussi

par cet afflux de sang bucolique
tandis que sur le seuil la muse en tablier,

pour couper court à de sombres soucis,
participe en criant: Attention

à ta chemise, l'herbe tache! (Au fond,
désespoir n'est pas si mal, c'est même

une espèce de consolation, le comprimé
du soir qui tombe sans un floc

dans le philtre des vieux amants.)

Construction-Site of the Elegy

I

Mowing the October lawn—the last
before the russet horde and the grip of winter,

despair (or what else if tomorrow
doesn't exist?) grips your throat

and it's not too much to say that one holds back tears
while stirring the green flour.

The machine beside you sputters bravely
as if it too were intoxicated

by this flow of bucolic blood
while on the threshold, the muse in an apron,

cutting short your dark reflections,
joins in, shouting "Watch out

for your shirt, grass stains!" (In the end,
despair's not so bad, it's even

a kind of consolation, the evening's
pill which drops without a splash

into the elixir of old lovers.)

II

(Et dire que le printemps pour nous
s'était marié sous l'aubépine en fleur,

que tout était paré pour un voyage
sans retour au cœur de l'éclaircie:

les toits rouges, l'échine bleuie
des collines et les arbres déjà

croisant leurs bras sur le ciel
comme si rien jamais plus

ne devait changer, malgré la pluie,
le vent, la grêle et la détresse

commune au musicien qui doute
en plein opéra d'aimer la musique

et de l'entendre, de la supporter encore,
et qui reste quand même assis

parmi les accessoires d l'élégie
comme ces statues au fond du parc

à tricoter du silence pour les dieux épuisés.

II

(And to think that for us, spring
was married beneath the flowering hawthorn,

that everything was decked out for a one-way
trip to the heart of the clearing:

the red roofs, the blued spine
of the hills, and the trees already

crossing their arms against the sky
as if nothing ever again

would change, despite the rain,
the wind, the hail, and the distress

shared by the musician who in the midst
of an opera doubts that he likes music

and still must hear it, must put up with it
and who remains seated nonetheless

among the elegy's accessories
like those statues at the far end of the park

knitting silence for the exhausted gods.

III

Dire que nous avons cru au bonheur
comme les gosses battant pavillon

sur un peu d'eau croupie dans l'arrière-cour
—ils savent qu'un rien suffirait

à renverser la mer sur sa quille,
mais font comme si en attendant

qu'une vague plus haute et qui blesse
leur enlève le goût

de tutoyer l'éternité. Nous aussi,
nous avons cru que la terre tournait

entre nos bras, et tournerait toujours
comme le soleil autour du pommier

—ô paisible torpeur, quand déjà
le ver était sous l'écorce,

affûtés les outils dans la remise ardente
et le sang bouillonnant dans les muscles

des équarrisseurs de rêves.

III

And to think that we believed in happiness
like kids flying their boat's flag

over a stagnant puddle in the alley
—they know that a breath would be enough

to spill the sea across its keel
but make believe while waiting

for a bigger wounding wave
to take away their taste for being

on first-name terms with eternity. We too,
we believed that the earth turned

in our arms, and would always turn
like the sun orbiting the apple-tree

—a peaceful torpor, when the worm
was already beneath the bark

the tools sharpened in the burning shed
and blood boiling in the muscles

of the dream-butchers.

IV

Mais la mort a passé sa main lourde
dans la chevelure des étés

et le dernier soleil a fait une torche
devant nous des oripeaux du tilleul,

éclaboussant de pourpre et d'or
le jardin fermé de notre amour

et nos yeux d'habitude, puis la brume
est venue, et tes larmes, et l'hiver

accrochant aux barbelés de l'horizon
la robe du premier bal, la robe

sans couture et la promesse non tenue
de changer l'eau des jours en vin,

de changer l'eau, chaque jour,
et la soif, et la mer,

l'amer visage du monde,
chaque jour

—en vain.

IV

But death has passed its heavy hand
through the thick hair of summers

and the last sun has made a torch
before us from the bright rags of the lime-tree

splashing with purple and gold as usual
the closed garden of our love

and our eyes, then the fog
came, and your tears, and winter

snagging on the horizon's barbed wire
the first ball-gown, the seamless

dress and the unkept promise
to change the water of our days to wine

to change the water, every day,
and thirst, and the sea,

the world's bitter face,
every day

—in vain.

V

C'est ainsi, soir après soir,
que nous sommes devenus mortels,

accusant la fatigue, le froid
et la distance des corps soudain

rendus à la pesanteur, comme si
la pomme en sa rondeur tenue

dans nos mains pâles, leur échappant,
avait éparpillé sur la terre

les restes en nous de l'ancien paradis.
C'est ainsi, nuit après nuit,

que nous sommes devenus seuls
comme les miroirs des chambres d'enfants

dans la maison expropriée: ouverts
sur la tapisserie des anges qui se décolorent,

et sans autre perspective désormais
que la démolition, pierre à pierre,

de ce qui fut aussi notre ciel
de lit, l'histoire sans fin

recommencée de l'amour ô flasque
otage du temps et de l'ennui)

V

This is how, evening after evening,
we became mortal

blaming fatigue, cold,
and the distance of bodies suddenly

exhausted into heaviness, as if
the apple in its roundness held

in our pale hands, escaping them
had scattered on the earth

what was left in us of the old paradise.
This is how, night after night

we became alone
like the mirrors in children's bedrooms

in a foreclosed house: facing
the fading angel wallpaper

and henceforth with no other future
but demolition, stone by stone

of what was also the canopy
above our bed, the story endlessly

repeated of love O flaccid
hostage of time and boredom)

VI

Que bourreau et victime à présent
se confondent ou s'effacent, la tâche

est faite et l'herbe rendue au dépotoir
qu'encensent les corbeaux,

et l'on peut désormais passer du billot
vert à la crémeuse corbeille des chambres

sans se laver les yeux car la tête
a déjà roulé quelque part

en versant son charroi de larmes
près du pommier qui carde l'horizon:

le corps est pris qui croyait prendre
et tenir l'amour unique entre ses bras

où tout est perte, tout, et finit
par s'écrouler comme un mur ou comme

ce vieux plant de chardon qui abîmait la faux.

Even if executioner and victim now
are merged or erased, the job

is done, and the grass brought to the dump
praised to the skies by crows,

and we can henceforth go from the headsman's
dollar-green block to the creamy basket of bedrooms

without washing our eyes since a head
has already rolled somewhere

spilling its tumbril of tears
close to the apple tree carding the horizon:

the body is taken which thought to take
and hold the one love in its arms

where all, all is loss, and ends up
collapsing like a wall or like

that old thistle-spike which blunted the scythe.

Pain de coucou
à Gérard Noiret

I

Comme partout ailleurs le ciel à Bezons
est par-dessus les toits, et peu s'inquiètent
en bas de la qualité d'une étoffe
si commune—sauf le vieux boxer peut-être

qui ne dort plus et rumine sa fin
prochaine à la fenêtre du troisième
Cité des Lilas tandis que les petits
pavillons de meulières font corps avec

le souvenir l'oubli des jours maigres et
du pain dur. C'était hier et ça reste
comme le ciel dans la mémoire, un bleu

de plus en plus rapiécé: le retour
de mon père à la maison et ses mains
nues et meurtries près de l'assiette à fleurs.

Cuckoo's Bread

to Gérard Noiret

I

Like anywhere else, the sky in Bezons
is up above the rooftops, and few below
bother themselves about the quality of such a
common stuff—except perhaps the old boxer

who can't sleep anymore and broods over
his approaching end at the third-floor window
in the Cité des Lilas while the little
millstone-pavilions are one with

remembering and forgetting lean days and
hard bread. That was yesterday and that remains
like a recalled sky, a more

and more patched-over blue: my father
coming home from work, his hands
bare and battered near the flowered plate.

La saveur qu'il garde encore ici, au détour
du chantier, le pain de coucou de mon père! c'est
comme le chant du désert, j'imagine, dans la voix
de la jeune Targui faisant voler le sable

du bac *Cité Victor Hugo*. Elle n'a pas
traversé la mer et ne sait rien du simoun,
mais le sable, voilà, c'est en elle, c'est elle
et la mer reste au fond, dans les vitres, les yeux

du vieux Kabyle sur le marché: ce petit pan
de bleu qui étincelle, la tendresse ou quoi d'autre?
Peut-être la joie d'entendre aux soirs de banlieue,

mêlés aux cris des martinets, et qui s'appellent
se répondent, ces noms de fleurs, de vent, de sable:
Hans, Idriss, Tonio, Marjolaine, Sarah.

What flavor it still keeps here, on my detour
around the worksite, my father's cuckoo's bread! It's
like the song of the desert, I imagine, in the voice
of the young Touareg making the sand fly

from the sandbox in the Cité Victor-Hugo. She has not
crossed the ocean and knows nothing about simoons,
but sand, there it is, it's in her, it is her
and the sea stays below it, in windowpanes, in the eyes

of the old Kabyle in the market: that little patch
of blue which sparkles, tenderness or what else?
Perhaps the joy of hearing, evenings, in the suburb,

mixed with swifts' cries, those who are called by,
who answer to, these names of flowers, of wind, of sand:
Hans, Idriss, Tonio, Marjolaine, Sarah.

Un Voile d'éther

Nous avons beau savoir que le ciel n'est rien
qu'une illusion pareille au bonheur quand tout va:
les p'tits bateaux au fil du temps, l'horizon
comme un archet ou comme

la hanche d'une femme dans les bras du sommeil,
tout, tout s'aigrit à la moindre occasion:
la vue d'une chambre étroite, d'une rangée
de peupliers sous la fenêtre

—les mêmes peupliers, la même fenêtre,
forme et fond de l'insupportable absence—
beau savoir, oui, que ce n'est qu'un voile d'éther
sur nos yeux blessés, c'est encore pour lui

que nous bradons l'espace et toutes les couleurs.

Le Noyer d'hiver

Mais il y a tante à faire et déjà le voisin
scie la forêt par cœur. Au pré les vaches boivent
le lait du ciel et les moineaux soignent le vent.

Il y a tant à faire et tout va se défait.
Le fil bleu de ta vie, dans quelle cuisine d'ombres
l'as-tu laissé se perdre, lui qui te menait doux

comme ces mots sans voix à l'envers des poèmes;
ou si c'est une femme là-bas derrière la mer
qui le porte à son doigt, et chacun de ses gestes

The Veil of Ether

It makes no difference that we know the sky is only
an illusion, like happiness when everything's going well:
the little boats as time passes, the horizon
like a flexed bow or like

the hip of a woman in the arms of sleep,
all, all goes sour at the least occasion:
the sight of a narrow room, of a row
of poplars under the window

—the same poplars, the same window,
form and content of an unbearable absence—
no difference, yes, that it's only a veil of ether
on our wounded eyes, it's still for the sky

that we bargain away space and all the colors.

The Winter Walnut-Tree

But there's so much to do, and already the neighbor
is sawing the forest by heart. In the field cows drink
the sky's milk and sparrows heal the wind.

There's so much to do and everything is undoing.
The blue thread of your life, in what kitchen of shadows
did you let it disappear, though it led you gently

like those voiceless words on a poem's overleaf;
or if there were a woman back behind the sea
who wears it on her finger, and each of her movements

—elle pose le café sur la table deux tasses
puis s'arrête, car elle est seule aussi—et chacun
de ses gestes rejoint ton front contre la vitre

qui regarde la mer monter à l'horizon
où il n'y a rien d'autre qu'un vieux noyer d'hiver
et qui étreint du bleu, et qui étreint du bleu.

L'Or Bleu

Non, les larmes n'arrêtent pas de couler
sur la terre, ni les cris de retentir.
Collines et cloisons nous défendent seulement
des corps qui vont avec et se défont

et les fleuves larges et paisibles, et les nuées
entraînent la douleur au loin. Mais à peine
la maison comme un mouchoir refermée
sur son carré d'amertume,

comme la tasse de café brûlant et le verre
de schnaps semblent soudain lourds!
Et si froide, inutile et petite la main
qui dilapidait la lumière sur ta peau

comme le ciel son or bleu sur la mer.

—she puts the coffee on the table two cups
then stops because she also is alone—and each
of her movements meets your forehead against the windowpane

watching the sea rise on the horizon
where there's nothing but an old winter walnut tree
which embraces the blue, which embraces the blue.

Blue Gold

No, tears don't stop flowing
on earth, nor cries resounding.
Hills and walls only protect us
from bodies that come with them and come undone

and the wide, peaceful rivers, and thunderclouds
carry grief away. But as soon
as the house is closed up like a handerkerchief
on its square of bitterness

how heavy the scalding cup of coffee and the glass
of schnapps suddenly seem!
And so cold, useless and small the hand
which squandered light on your skin

like the sky wasting its blue gold on the sea.

Les dernières pièces
à Jacques Borel

Comme ceux qui crurent un jour dépasser l'horizon
et qui, le geste las, ne parlent plus qu'avec leur chien,

tu répètes que le bonheur est plein de vide
et qu'on a beau crier contre les murs sournois,

l'herbe demeure le chemin le plus tendre
vers l'abattoir—et le boucher peut encore

caresser sa femme avec des mains de soie.
Et tu cries, oui tu cries, mais de plus en plus bas:

bonheur, bonheur, comme on jette,
couché sur la margelle du ciel,

ses dernières pièces dans le bleu qui bouge:
ces yeux que rien ne comble plus

sinon dans la nuit des amants outragés
la sourde et lente montée des larmes.

The Last Coins
to Jacques Borel

Like those who thought one day they'd cross the horizon
and who now with weary gestures talk only to the dog,

you repeat that happiness is full of holes
and there's no use crying out against the cunning walls,

the grass is still the gentlest path
to the slaughterhouse—and the butcher can

still caress his wife with silken hands.
And you cry out, cry out, but more and more softly:

happiness, happiness, as you would throw,
stretched out on the edge of the sky,

your last coins into the moving blue:
those eyes which nothing satisfies any more

if not, in the night of offended lovers,
a slow and soundless upswelling of tears.

Emmaüs

Le soleil du soir en été calme le jeu
de la mort qui plante son dard
partout, dans la sueur et l'écrasement
de midi. Au ras de l'herbe sans bruit,

la coccinelle fait une dernière promenade
tandis que les autos passent en douce
de petites médailles jaunes au revers
de la colline qui se déshabille.

Assis, tu contemples tes pieds nus,
désormais affranchis des sentes et détachés
de toi, comme ces inconnus qui ont porté
la charge du jour et qui demandent

pourquoi, s'il faut mourir encore.

Emmaüs

The evening sun in summer calms the game
of death which drives its dart
in everywhere in the sweat and crush
of noon. Level with the noiseless

grass, the ladybug takes a last stroll
while cars pass quietly
little yellow medals on the lapel
of the hill which is undressing.

Seated, you contemplate your bare feet
henceforth free from footpaths and detached
from you, like those strangers who carried
the day's load, and who ask

why, if they still must die.

Quatre saisons pour Jude Stéfan

Automne

La vie nulle sous le grimoire des noms,
c'est nous à l'enseigne déjà des futurs
trépassés, nous encore dans l'âcre odeur
des feuilles jaunies que la mer

en ce fumeux lointain condense, nous
qui rêvons de partir, oiseaux prostrés
sur la corde du vide accrochant
la nuit des chambres à celle des désirs,

et que rompt d'un seul coup, à la fenêtre
du réveil, le corps buté de la terre
prise par le gel. Ô chrysanthèmes, rendez
à nos âmes dégrisées un peu de la couleur

des femmes qui passent en riant.

Hiver

I

L'hospice accoté au collège et déjà
chacun de nous marquant sa place d'affamé
vieillard dans les trous de la haie, l'œil
fauve strié de lames grises (ô cyprès)

Four Seasons for Jude Stéfan

Autumn

Life useless under the scribble of names
it's us already beneath the banner of deceased
futures, us again in the bitter smell
of yellow leaves that the sea

is condensing in this hazy distance, we
who dream of leaving, despondent birds
on the cord of emptiness connecting
the night of bedrooms to the one of desire,

which breaks all at once, at the window
of waking, the stubborn body of the earth
seized by frost. O chrysanthemums, give back
to our sobered bodies a bit of the color

of women who pass by laughing.

Winter

I

The nursing home leans on the boarding-school and already
each of us marks his place as a starving
ancient through the gaps in the hedge, tawny
eye striped with gray blades (O cypress)

—et de larmes bientôt quand l'autobus
aura passé, quand, la cellule refermée
comme un poing sur l'encaustique et la mâle
odeur, la mort se couchera

toute nue contre nous, marquant
sa place elle aussi ô jalouse des corps
qui tant s'allumèrent, tant (et si vite
s'éteignent) aux jambes gainées d'orages

des Suzannes de quinze ans.

II

À tout va, fol amour, à l'eau qui pleure
sur la vitre en ce décembre sans arroi
de blancs manteaux (mais non sans griserie),
à tout va, au déclin des fiers grands arbres

auréolés d'enfance où nous tenions vigie
longtemps sur les plats villages comme
assiettes pilées dans la verte marée des vals:
ils sont couchés au fond de nous à présent

comme la mer, et qui les relèvera, qui
si l'amour n'est autre que vague furieuse
retombante, quand nous voudrions qu'il soit
comme un soc dans la terre d'oubli recru,

un soc arrachant l'ivraie d'avenir.

—and with tears soon enough when the bus
will have passed, when, the cell closed up
like a fist on the floor-wax and the male
odor, death will lie down

naked among us, marking
a place as well, O jealous of bodies
which so lit up, so (and so swiftly
fizzled out) at the storm-stockinged legs

of fifteen-year-old Susannas.

II

Everything staked, mad love, on water which weeps
on the pane this December, with no retinue
of white-robed monks (but not without exhilaration),
everything staked, on the waning of tall proud trees

haloed with childhood where for hours
we would stand vigil over the flat villages like
heaped plates in the green tides of valleys:
they lie in our depths now

like the sea, and who will raise them, who
if love is nothing but a wild wave
falling, when we would have wished it
like a ploughshare in the earth of exhausted forgetfulness,

a ploughshare uprooting the chaff of the future.

Printemps

I

Recommencer, naître à nouveau, voilà
ce que disait le Maître, ce que nous
n'avions pas compris. Nous regardions
le ventre de la terre, les nuages, le ciel

et demeurions aveugles, tandis que l'hirondelle
revenait à sa place exacte, reprenait
possession du vent. Et nous qui de si loin
désirions partir, nous restons sur le seuil

sans savoir où aller, comme prisonniers
d'une route invisible et de la peur de perdre,
en plongeant dans la lumière d'avril,
le goût de l'eau, le parfum des ombres

et le plaisir de toujours remettre à demain.

II

Mais demain est un mot qui n'a pas d'avenir
sur l'échelle du vent. Regarde ta chienne
alanguie dans l'herbe: elle va mourir
et dans ses yeux voilés la lumière

immobile frémit, caresse du présent
qui passe. Le temps pour elle est une maison
vide, qui flotte dans l'écuelle du chat.
Ouvre la porte: elle applaudit

Spring

To begin again, to be reborn, that's
what the Master really said, which we
did not understand. We would look at
the earth's belly, at the clouds, the sky

and remain blind, while the swallow
returned to the selfsame place, resumed
possession of the wind. And we, who would have so
preferred to depart, we stay on the threshold

not knowing where to go, like prisoners
of an invisible map, and of the fear of losing,
while diving into the April light,
the taste of water, the perfume of shadows

and the pleasure of always putting off till tomorrow.

But tomorrow is a word with no future
on the wind's scale. Look at your dog
languorous on the grass: she is going to die
and in her shadowed eyes the motionless

light trembles, a caress of the passing
present. Time for her is an empty
house, which floats in the cat's bowl.
Open the door: she applauds

de tout son corps difforme et laid.
Elle n'attend rien hors de ton ombre,
ne possédant rien, sauf cette image de toi
qui agrandit d'un coup l'espace

et fait rebondir la terre, à ton appel.

Été

Dévore, feu, beau feu aux langues de démones
tous ces papiers, ces livres, ces lettres mortes,
et le vieil homme plein de rancœur et plein
de nuit, dévore-le

avec le mauvais drame de sa vie, cette vieille
partition à une seule main sur la scène du cœur
tandis que l'autre dans la coulisse bat le vide,
cherchant quoi? un amour

qui ne ferme pas à clef les battants
de l'horizon, mais porte plus haut que nous
ses flammes dans le soir qui s'étire: amour
qui te ressemble feu,

mais comme une pierre dans la paume de midi.

with her whole misshapen ugly body.
All she waits for is your shadow,
owning nothing, except that image of you
which swells space in an instant

and sets the earth in motion at your call.

Summer

Devour, fire, lovely fire with she-demon's tongues
all these papers, these books, these dead letters
and the old man full of rancor and full
of night, devour him

with the bad play of his life, that old
score for one hand on the heart's stage
while the other one saws the air in the wings
seeking what? a love

which doesn't lock the shutters
of the horizon, but bears its flames
up above us in the spreading dusk: love
which resembles you, fire

but like a stone in the palm of noon.

Dilectures Predilectures

Variations sur une montée en tramway
(d'après une photo attribuée à J. H. Lartigue, 1900)

I

Assis à l'arrière, à contre-sens et fumaillant
dans le jour frais, il a vivement tourné la tête

vers l'inconnue qui sautait dans le tramway
en marche, une main relevant la jupe et

découvrant le mollet rond et la cheville
serrés dans la bas noir. Il a tout vu, tout

senti, tout entendu: la vivacité de l'ablette
dans le courant, la saveur du premier

fruit dérobé à l'étalage, et comme
la verge de coudrier sifflait dans l'air

quand elle allait s'abattre sur son dos
d'enfant, mais à l'heure de parler d'elle

aux amis curieux et qui riaient d'avance,
plus rien, ni grâce, ni éclat, mais des mots

comme les papiers gras sur l'herbe après la fête,
quand l'ombre s'allonge et nous glace le cœur.

Boarding the Streetcar: Variations
(after a photograph attributed to J. H. Lartigue, 1900)

I

Seated towards the rear, facing backwards, smoking
in the cool day, he briskly turned his head

toward the stranger, who jumped onto the moving
streetcar, one hand holding her skirt up and

uncovering her rounded calf and ankle
clasped in a black stocking. He saw everything, felt

and heard everything: the swift brightness of minnows
in a current, the taste of the first

fruit swiped from a market-stall, and how
the hazel switch whistled in the air

when it was about to strike a child's
back, but when he might have talked about it

to his friends, curious and already laughing,
nothing, no grace, no spark, only words

like paper littering the grass after a fair
when shadows as they lengthen chill our hearts.

Le contrôleur n° 559, n'a vu que le danger
encouru par la belle et déjà sa main droite

a lâché l'ombre pour la proie. Trop tard,
l'intrépide est à bord, un pied sur la marche,

l'autre encore dans le vide, traînant
la pointe de l'escarpin sur la terre qui bouge.

C'est assez pour que le voyageur se retourne,
remonte la couture du bas jusqu'à la nuque

d'herbe tendre que broute un chapeau cloche.
S'il sut jamais rien du visage d'albâtre,

de la bouche cerise et des yeux agrandis,
il emporta cela qui fait battre longtemps

le sang des choses comme un cœur
dans l'ombre des chambres mortes:

l'effroi de la rose ébouriffée, la cendre
de toutes les promesses dans le tiroir

du temps, la mort qui vient
à notre rencontre et ne se retourne pas.

Conductor #559 saw only the danger
the beauty was incurring and his right hand had already

loosed its bird to seize this prey. Too late,
the intrepid one is on board, one foot on the step,

the other one still in empty air, dragging
the toe of her pump on the moving ground.

That's enough to make the traveler turn his head
and ascend the seam of her stocking up to her grass-

tender nape which a cloche hat grazes.
If he never knew the alabaster face,

the cherry lips and the widened eyes,
he still took something away which makes

the blood of things beat lengthily like a heart
in the shadow of dead rooms:

the terror of the tousled rose, the ashes
of every promise in the drawer

of time, death which is coming
to meet us and doesn't turn back.

Borges

Un jour, la nuit s'établira sur toutes choses
et bonheur et malheur pourront se regarder
droit dans les yeux car les miroirs auront cessé
d'opposer l'homme à son vain reflet. Le tigre,
même à l'ombre des barreaux, connaîtra que nulle
est la gloire des livres; qu'au mythique héros
des contes populaires, l'or inaltérable
fut enlevé, et qu'il leste à présent sa proie
frileuse mais digne dans le vent du combat.
Tel qui se croyait aveugle, timide, sans
courage, descendit aux enfers, épousa
Béatrice et, tendant sa gorge au vieux rasoir
du Temps, affronta l'autre, ce double inconnu
derrière la porte, qui fait saigner les roses.

Borges

One day, night will settle over everything
and joy and sorrow will be able to look each other
straight in the eye because mirrors will have ceased
setting us up against our vain reflections. The tiger,
even in the cage-bars' shadow, will know that fame
that comes from books is null; that the pure gold was taken
from the folk-tale hero, and that he's now gobbling down his prey
chilled but worthy in the wind of combat.
He who thought himself blind, timid, lacking
courage, descended into hell, married
Beatrice, and, baring his throat to the old razor-blade
of Time, faced up to the other, that unknown double
behind the door, who made the roses bleed.

Le Voyageur oublié
(Sur un vers de Claude Roy)

C'est la vie qui nous fait mourir,
écriviez-vous dans ce poème où tout
demeure à vif: le crépitement des trolleys,
la nuque de l'amante à son miroir

et jusqu'à la jeune morte sur son lit,
tellement sage qu'on ne sait plus
si c'est le temps qui passe ou nous
qui passons à travers lui, les mains vides,

comme un train somnambule à travers
la campagne endormie—et le voyageur
oublié dans le creux de ses bras

est un lac au soleil de midi, un lac
que rien ne trouble, pas même le reflet
du corps penché qui tremble dans la vitre.

À Cavafy

Que d'impatience et pour quoi si demain
n'est qu'une barque sans voile ni rame,
un pont sur le vide? Pense au vieil homme
d'Alexandrie, à ses trésors enfouis

dans un tiroir parmi les clefs, un reste
de tabac, le profil usé d'un roitelet déchu.
Il suffisait d'un klaxon dans la rue,
d'un pas plus vif dans l'escalier

The Forgotten Traveler
(on a line by Claude Roy)

It's life itself that makes us die,
you wrote in that poem where everything
gapes raw, the streetcars' rattling,
the nape of a lover's neck at her mirror

and even the young corpse in her bed,
so well-behaved we no longer know
if it's time which passes or we ourselves
who pass across it, empty-handed

like a train sleepwalking across
the dozing countryside—and the traveler
forgotten in the crook of its arms

is a lake in the noon sun, a lake
troubled by nothing, not even the reflection
of his bent body trembling in the window.

To Cavafy

Such impatience, and for what, if tomorrow
is only a little boat with no sail or oars,
a bridge over nothing? Think of the old man
of Alexandria, of his treasures squirreled

away in a drawer with keys, leftover flakes of
tobacco, the weary portrait of a deposed princeling.
All it took was a car-horn honking in the street,
a livelier step on the stairway.

pour réveiller la chambre, le corps voluptueux
de l'ange, la cinglante et fragile
beauté de l'amour, et sa voix dans le noir
comme du sel

jeté sur une plaie, en passant.

À Georges Perros au piano
pour Michel Butor

Les oiseaux, oui, qui n'ont pas de dents,
pas de doutes, pas de regrets, et les enfants
qui trainent la mer au bout d'une ficelle,
et les femmes dont le *non* est un oui

dans une autre gamme, quand on a le dos
au sol et que leur ombre dans nos yeux
verse à pleins seaux le ciel qui toujours
lève l'ancre à nos genoux,

et les poètes que la vie traverse
comme un train l'affiche bleue des voyages
—et chaque vers sous l'ecchymose
porte le chiffre de la rose et du

déchirante bonheur d'être nu parmi les ronces.

to wake up the room, the angel's voluptuous
body, the knife-sharp fragile
beauty of love, and his voice in the darkness
like salt

thrown on a wound, in passing.

To Georges Perros at the Piano
for Michel Butor

Birds, of course, who have no teeth,
no doubts, no regrets, and children
who pull the sea along at the end of a string,
and women whose *no* is a yes

in another key, when our backs
are pinned to the ground and their shadows pour
into our eyes those bucketsful of sky which always
lifts anchor at our knees

and poets whom life crosses
as a train crosses the blue poster of journeys
—and beneath the bruise each line
bears the seal of the rose and of the

piercing joy at being naked in the thorns.

Max Jacob

Priez pour le petit saltimbanque à croix
jaune, qui enviait le crapaud, priez

pour lui qui fut ange aux jours de défaite et
bête au laboratoire de l'échanson.

Cyprien là, Max ici, pitre qui crâne
comme un œuf sous le chapeau et pleure sans,

pleure sang et eau les cent plaies du Seigneur
et puis change de peau, noir à Paris, blanc

à Saint-Benoît et arc-en-ciel à Drancy
pour célébrer la messe de l'Arlequin

qui ouvre le paradis. Priez pour Max,
roi de Boétie et prince des poètes

qui tant pria pour nous, répétant qu'un sein
peut toujours en cacher un autre, que sous

le masque une seule vérité se terre,
la même: *Nous allons mourir tout à l'heure.*

Max Jacob

Pray for the little acrobat with the yellow
cross, who envied a toad, pray

for him, an angel on days of defeat and
the wine waiter's lab rat

Cyprien there, Max here, a clown who's bold
as an egg beneath his hat and weeps when bald

weeps blood and water all the Saviour's wounds
and then switches skins, black in Paris, white

in St-Benoît, a rainbow at Drancy
to celebrate the harlequin's mass

which opens Paradise. Pray for Max
king of Boetia and prince of poets

who prayed so much for us, repeating that one breast
may hide another, that beneath

the mask there's only one truth hidden,
the same one: *We'll all die sooner or later.*

Yannis Ritsos
pour Eleanna et Gilles

Les montagnes, les maisons, les arbres
et la grande cour vide et noyée

de soleil. Il suffirait d'un nom
prononcé à voix basse: Hélène ou

Perséphone, pour que la mer sorte
de l'ombre du figuier, que revienne

à nouveau la petite charrette
pleine d'algues, de débris, derrière

la mule aux yeux clos. Il suffirait
d'un simple mot pour que les monts s'en

aillent un par un en silence tels
les rivaux d'Ulysse, et que les arbres

surpris par l'incendie des fenêtres
se changent en statues, cependant

qu'au milieu du brasier grandit l'ombre
d'un homme à sa table, indifférent

aux flammes, et gravant avec un
vieux canif, sur l'éclat de soleil

rapporté de Yaros, ce que nul
dieu ni tyran ne disputera

jamais à l'aveugle, à la veuve, à
la mère: les lumineuses larmes.

Yannis Ritsos

for Eleanna and Gilles

The mountains, the houses, the trees
and the wide courtyard, empty and drowned

in sunlight. It would only take a name
uttered in a low voice: Helen or

Persephone, for the sea to emerge
from the fig tree's shadow, for the little cart

to come back, loaded
with seaweed and debris, behind

the mule with closed eyes. It would only take
a simple word for the hills to

depart, one by one, silently, like
Ulysses' rivals, and for the trees

astonished by the windows' conflagration
to turn to statues, while

in the midst of the flames grows the shadow
of a man at his table, indifferent

to the fire, and carving with an
old penknife, on the blaze of sunlight

brought back from Yaros something no
god nor tyrant would ever

deny to the blind man, the widow,
the mother: luminous tears.

Poète en Groningue
pour Rutger Kopland

Songer à partir, disait-il, et c'était encore
sous les mots du poème comme une barque
quand le soleil se noie au milieu du lac,
juste là où le vent n'élargit plus

les cercles, une barque frêle et qui
fait mine de vouloir s'en aller, va, revient,
et l'eau proteste contre la proue, et personne
pour comprendre et traduire cela :

que de si petites vagues—rêves, souvenirs
—aient toujours raison de nos plus fiers
élans, de nos désirs d'échapper au reflux.
Personne, sinon celui qui parle de partir

et cherche encore *un endroit pour rester*

À la mémoire de W. H. Auden
(mort en septembre 1973)
pour Marilyn Hacker

I

Ce qui est grave, ce n'est pas de n'avoir
qu'un manteau de fortune, une seule paire

de chaussures éreintées quand il neige
et que le vent froid souffle en rafales

ni que la plomberie dans la chambre soit aussi
pourrie que les bronches du fumeur, les artères

Poet in Gröningen
for Rutger Kopland

Imagine leaving, he'd say, and it stayed
beneath the poem's words, like an open boat
when the sun drowns itself in the middle of the lake
just there where the wind no longer spreads

its circles, a frail skiff and one which
pretends to want to go, departs, comes back
and the water protests against its prow, and no one
there to understand and translate this:

how such minuscule waves—dreams, memories
—always get the best of our proudest
surges, our desire to escape the backwash.
No one, except the one who talks of leaving

and still is looking for *a place to stay*

In Memory of W. H. Auden
(died September 1973)
for Marilyn Hacker

I

What matters is not possessing only
a threadbare coat, a single pair

of run-over shoes when it snows
not that the cold wind blusters

nor that the pipes in your room are as
rotten as a smoker's lungs, the roadways

des villes bombardées, les paroles des faux
prophètes et les promesses des gouvernants

ni que le marchand de vin refuse
obstinément tout nouveau crédit

alors que l'eau du robinet a le goût
du rat crevé, ni que le ciel s'éloigne

à mesure que nous grandissons, et la terre
tout à coup colle à nos pieds, l'ombre

qui nous suivait bientôt nous distance
et c'est la nuit comme un voleur, fracassant

le regard du voyageur arrêté
au milieu des valises, qui emporte

avec la clef du paysage la route et
la soif et le sel de vivre. Ce qui est grave,

disait-il, c'est d'avoir oublié que l'homme,
secoué par les vagues d'ennuis divers

et de détresse, est plus vaste et profond
que la mer mais plus fragile

que feuille d'automne si, dressé
contre lui-même dans la prison du corps

battu, il ne sait plus rendre grâce
au présent *pour la vie qui fleurit*

sur un visage ou flambe comme une rose.

of bombed-out cities, the words of false
prophets, the promises of politicians

nor that the liquor-store manager subbornly
refuses you any more purchases on credit

while the tap-water tastes
of dead rat, nor that the sky gets further

away the taller we grow, and the earth
suddenly sticks to our feet, the shadow

which followed us catches up and passes
and there's night, like a thief, shattering

the stare of the traveler stopped short
amidst his suitcases, which carries off

along with the key to the country the road and
the thirst and the spice of life. What matters

he said, is to have forgotten that man,
shaken by the blasts of sundry distresses

and anguish, is vaster and deeper
than the sea and nonetheless more fragile

than a fallen leaf if, propped up
against himself within the beaten

body's prison, he no longer can pay homage
to the present, *for life which flowers*

on a face or flames up like a rose.

II

We must love one another or die! w. h. auden

Pour lui, la chose survint à Vienne
comme un coup de poignard ou la tenture

rouge qu'une fille d'étage intempestive
tire violemment dans la chambre close

de ses bras, et nul n'a pu confondre
son cri avec le contre-ut du chanteur

d'opéra qui répétait derrière
la cloison, ni avec le grincement

du tramway sur le ring à deux pas
de la Walfischgasse où les balayeurs

poursuivaient leur valse nonchalante
entre les feuilles mortes et les vieux

tickets. Seul avec ses pieds, comme
il disait, le poète a fichu le camp

sans fermer sa valise, car tout,
comme le plus beau vers, demeure

inachevé ici bas, en attente
d'une autre bouche, d'un autre accord,

selon qu'il est écrit que *pour faire Un
il faut être Deux*, que l'amour seul

unit et le reste est déconfiture.

II

We must love one another or die! W. H. AUDEN

For him, the event occurred in Vienna
like a dagger-thrust or the red

draperies which an over-zealous chambermaid
pulls violently shut in the closed room

of his arms, and no one could have confused
his cry with the C-sharp of the opera

singer rehearsing on the other side
of the wall, nor with the screech

of the trolley on the Ring two steps from
the Walfischgasse where the street-sweepers

continued their nonchalant waltz
among the dead leaves and discarded

bus tickets. Alone with his feet, as
he put it, the poet packed off

without shutting his suitcase, since everything,
even the loveliest line, remains

unfinished here below, waiting
for another mouth, another harmony,

where it is written that *for there to be One
there must be Two*, that love alone

connects and the rest is rout.

Lettre à Félicien Rops
(à propos de *Pornokratès* ou la dâme au cochon)
pour Hédi Kaddour

a

Avant que mort me fonde
luxurieusement
comme l'or blet des feuilles
en ce septembre mil
neuf cent quatre-vingt treize
le quarante-sixième
de ma banale vie
avant qu'elle m'arrache
aux lèvres des bacchantes
qui enciellent mon lit
et me jettent aux Parques
avant que tout soit dit

b

laissez-moi cher Fély
revenir en vos chambres
d'ébauches   ranimer
sous l'ocre scapulaire
des vélins et des arches
l'ancienne foi des saintes
qui sont nues   prendre encore
le parti de la chair
qui tant s'use et si vite
laissez-moi reverdir
comme un ciel à quatre heures
quand les orages ont fui

Letter to Félicien Rops
(concerning *Pornokratès*, or the lady with the pig)
for Hédi Kaddour

a

Before death melts me down
lasciviously
like leaves' overripe gold
in this September nine-
teen hundred ninety-three
the forty-sixth year of
my ordinary life
before death snatches me
from the Bacchantes' lips
who enheaven my bed
and throw me to the Fates
before all has been said

b

allow me, dear Fély
to re-enter your rooms
of sketches   to revive
beneath the ochre vel-
lum vestments and arches
the ancient faith of female
saints, stark naked,   take
the flesh's side again
so well worn-out so fast
let me re-green myself
like a four o'clock sky
after the storms have passed

c

et puis rouvrir le champ
du désir à la bête
(comme disent cagots
prévôts tous grands bouilleurs
de fange en l'auge des
confessionnaux   tous porcs
médaillés de *porno-*
kratès la belle aux yeux
bandés) oui, laissez-moi
réveiller soulever
vos merveilles à tresses
vos Flamandes à chiens
y délacer mes reins

d

Que Didons ménagères
petites mains folâtres
fortes et vacantes veuves
et goulues gourgandines
qui endormez le feu
dans des bras de linon
rose ou bleu et des jambes
enrésillées d'orages
me fondiez à mon tour
comme l'or des étés
au blanc creuset des cuisses
et le diable m'emporte

c

and re-open desire's
pastures to the beast
(so say the hypocrites
provosts, home-brewers of
filth in the trough of the
confessionals   prize pigs
ribbons pinned on by *Porno-
kratès*   the blindfolded
beauty) yes, allow me
to arouse, to enjoin
your long-braided treasures
your Flemish girls with dogs
and there unloose my loins.

d

You housewifely Didos
frolicsome little hands
underemployed stout widows
and gluttonous hussies
who put the fire to sleep
in pink or blue-dyed lawn
and linen arms and legs
netted in snoods of storms
melt me down in my turn
like summers' gold in the
white crucible of thighs
and let the devil take me

e

le diable et ses suivantes
si nous buvons ensemble
la gloire du Léthé
car c'est ainsi Fély
que je voudrais mourir
pinceau dans la peinture
des cambrures et des
poses   roide et nu comme
un if bleu à l'enseigne
des dames   Qu'au nectar
mêlée la sueur jette
sur nos ébats rupestres

f

le feu de la palette
des dieux   et tel un ru
de lumière mon beau
désordre et ma folie
s'en aillent en chantant
vers l'oubli sous la mousse
comme la feuille au vent
qui passe et nous disper-
sera tous chastes ou non
cendres parmi les fleurs
paisibles ou dessous
nourrissant à longueur

e

the devil and his girlfriends
if we drink together
to the glory of Lethe
because that, dear Fély
is how I'd like to die
brush in the paint-pot
of curves crevices poses
as stiff and naked as
a blue yew at those ladies'
shop-sign   Mingled with our
nectar let sweat spurt on
our frolics on the rocks

f

the flame of the gods'
palette   and like a brook
of light my beautiful
disorder and my madness
go off singing towards
forgetfulness beneath
the moss a wind-blown leaf
which passes and will dis-
perse us all chaste or not
cinders among the peaceful
flowers or beneath them
nourishing for the length

g

de nuits et de racines
les fabuleuses croupes
des collines fardées
de coquelicots   Que là
où vont nos sœurs les vaches
saouler l'alme mamelle
se renversent pour nous
les nues   Ô tubéreuse
langueur des asphodèles
pour l'apprenti gisant
qu'encore un temps je suis
couché entre mes bras

h

En attendant Fély
(car rien ne presse rien)
si la beauté est notre
seule chaire où prêcher
que la vie est unique
l'amour luxurieux
prêchons-y péchons-y
que ma dernière nuit
reste la plus gironde
entre toutes vos femmes
Pour l'heure laissez-moi
baiser votre main sur

i

les lèvres du printemps.

g

of nights and of roots
the fabulous rumps
of hills smeared with the rouge
of poppies   That there
where our sisters the cows
refill nourishing teats
for us the skies will roll
on their backs   O tuberous
languor of asphodels
for the apprentice tomb-
sculpture that I still am
recumbent in my arms

h

and while waiting Fély
(there is no hurry, none)
if beauty is the only
pulpit from which we preach
that there is just one life
and love is laced with lust
let's preach our sin, let's sin
so that my final night
will be the most curvaceous
of all your buxom women
For now simply allow
me to kiss your hand

i

upon the lips of spring.

Le Relèvement d'Icare

(D'après *Paysage avec la chute d'Icare*, de Breugel)

The Raising of Icarus

(After Breughel's *Landscape with the Fall of Icarus*)

Prologue

pour Yves Bergeret

Si j'ai vraiment vécu cette vie ou bien
seulement rêvassé dans la lumière
qui baigne ce bureau sous la mer des toits,

si c'est ma lampe seule qui brouillait
les signes en chemin, ou la fatigue encore
d'attendre que la pluie cesse

sa vaine dactylographie sur la vitre,
qui peut le dire et qui me refuser
d'avoir un jour marché sur la mer,

renversé le blue qui lave les oiseaux
et dilapidé l'or du tremble avec le mort
en cachette des voisins? Qui

sinon cet étranger en moi comme un enfant
courant après son ombre, mains tendues
mais l'âme plus courbée que celle du prodigue

soignant ses porcs dans la maison d'exil.

Prologue
for Yves Bergeret

If I've really lived this life or if
I've only daydreamed it in the light
which bathes my desk beneath the sea of roofs,

if it's my solitary lamp which scrambled
the signs along the way, or being tired
again of waiting for the rain to stop

its vain stenography against the panes
who can say and who can deny
that one day I walked on the sea,

spilled out the blue that washes the birds
and squandered the aspen's gold with a dead man
without the neighbors noticing? Who

besides this stranger in me like a child
running after his shadow, hands outstretched
but with his soul more stooped than the prodigal's

tending his swine in the house of exile.

Au fond du labyrinthe

I

Je me souviens: tous passaient en courant
dans le couloir du métro, à gauche à droite,
tirant tirés, pressés pressant, et comme
dévorés par leur ombre. Ils couraient

les uns contre les autres, même visage même
nuit, et chacun était la nuit de l'autre
et tous comme les oiseaux foudroyés
que la tempête entraîne

vers l'étrave des forêts mortes, tous
comme un seul s'enfonçaient en eux-mêmes
dans ce grenier encombré de gravats
et de morts, où trône et triomphe

le grand miroir blanc des aveugles.

II

L'un d'eux parfois levait un bras lourd
et c'était comme l'appel d'un noyé,
l'ultime tentative pour saisir
au-dessus des remous de la foule

le fil invisible qui lui eût rapporté
des profondeurs du temps un éclat de sa vie
ou le sens de la terre en cet instant
que tout se défigure et prend une autre voix,

In the Depths of the Labyrinth

I

I remember: they all went past me running
through the subway corridors, to the left to the right
pulling and pulled, pushing and pushed, as if
devoured by their own shadows. They were running

against each other, same face same
night, and each one was night for every other
and all of them like stunned birds
dragged in a storm's wake

towards the prow of dead forests, all, as one
man, sank into themselves
in that attic littered with rubble
and corpses, where, in triumph,

the vast white mirror of the blind presides.

II

Sometimes one of them would lift a heavy arm
and it was like a drowning man's appeal
the last attempt to grasp
above the backwash of the crowd

the unseen thread which would have brought him
a spark of his life up from the depths of time
or the way the earth turned in that instant
when everything blights itself, takes another voice,

mais toujours comme la vague brutale
une rame bondée rejetait le pêcheur
parmi les ombres soulevées sur la rive,
les vivants et les morts, vite

qui se retournent dans la poussière des jours.

III

Et tous ainsi continuaient leur course, tête
baissée comme après la débâcle ou pareils
aux bêtes sous le joug, poursuivant
dans le dessin d'un pas, le sillon d'une affiche,

Dieu sait quelle trace du bonheur interrompu,
la maille des premiers jours peut-être
quand le ciel se confondait avec la terre, leur corps
avec celui des arbres et leurs paroles

avec la voix des dieux—Souviens-toi, disaient-ils
pour eux-mêmes, souviens-toi quand nous mangions
de tous les fruits sans amertume et comme
nous chantions d'un même souffle avec les oiseaux.

—Je me souviens seulement d'un ciel sans fond.

but each time like a brutal wave
the packed train threw the fisherman back
among the shadows heaved up on the bank,
the living and the dead, quickly

turning over in the dust of days.

III

And so they all continued their race, heads
lowered as after a rout or like
beasts in a yoke, pursuing
in a footstep's shape, the furrow of a poster,

God knows what trace of interrupted joy,
perhaps the weave of their earliest days
when the sky merged with the earth, their own bodies
with those of trees and their words

with the voices of the gods—Do you remember, they mumbled
to themselves, do you remember when we would eat
of all fruits without bitterness and how
we sang with the same breath as the birds.

—I only remember a bottomless sky.

IV

Embarquer sans retour, voilà ce qu'ils voulaient,
jeter leur montre dans le premier jardin venu
et n'avoir plus qu'à contempler le ciel
comme le berger relevant des yeux

le garçon tombé dans l'eau verte. Nous n'avons
qu'une route et nos pieds n'y peuvent
rien, pensaient-ils. Icare est mort, et Bruegel,
et nous-mêmes, comme en marche vers Ninive,

bouche close, message oublié, cherchant
ce qu'il faudrait dire et à qui parler,
nous ne sommes plus qu'une trace déjà
dans la nuit, la retombée d'un songe

entre les rails du présent, et qui s'efface.

V

Mais le silence aussi comme le vent
après l'orage tombait derrière les rames
entraînant l'espace où tout était possible,
et les yeux se perdaient ainsi

entre les rails sans que personne fît un geste.
Les portières seules criaient encore
en se fermant: changez de vie—mais eux
déjà ne voyaient plus qu'un cheval

IV

To embark and not return is what they wanted,
to toss their watches over the first garden wall
and have nothing more to do than study the sky
like the shepherd raising with his eyes

the boy fallen into green water. We have only
one way to go and our feet can do nothing
about it, they thought. Icarus is dead, and Brueghel,
and we might be marching toward Nineveh,

our mouths closed, messages forgotten, searching
for what to say and whom to say it to,
we are no more than a mark already
made on the night, a dream deflating

between the moment's rails, disappearing.

V

But silence also dropped, like the wind
after a storm, behind the train
sweeping away the space where all was possible
and so their eyes meandered off

between the tracks without anyone budging.
Only the subway doors were still crying out
as they closed: change your life—but all
they could see now was a horse

à bout de course, un cheval et qui s'effondre,
et le cavalier au visage surpris,
posant sa tempe contre la vitre obscure,
c'était bien eux, et c'était bien la même terre

froide, et se dérobant sous leurs pieds.

Reproches au berger

Facile de prendre appui sur la lumière, disaient-ils,
pour qui n'a pas mission d'éblouir en tirant l'épée
ni souci de gagner sur d'autres rives l'or et les vivats
des foules, et le pain sans sueur, et la mort

glorieuse, mais charge seulement de quelques âmes
sourdes et lentes sous le ciseau des lunes. Facile
de ne pas peser plus qu'une larme d'enfant
sur le monde, un verbe de poète

tandis que nous partageons l'ombre avec le marchand,
le bourreau. Facile de rendre au ciel la monnaie
des yeux, la couronne de roses au couchant
et le sang des feuilles quand c'est nous

qui portons le royaume d'Icare à bout de bras.

at the end of a race, a horse collapsing,
there is the rider with an astonished face,
pressing his brow against the darkened window,
they were like that, and it was the same cold

earth, giving way beneath their feet.

The Shepherd Reproached

Easy enough to lean on the light, they said,
if you're not sworn to dazzle by drawing your sword
or concerned with winning gold elsewhere, and the cheers
of the crowd, and bread without sweat, and a glorious

death, but are merely in charge of a few slow, deaf
souls under the shears of the moon. Easy
to weigh the world down no more than a child's
tear, or a poet's verb

while we share the shadows with merchants
and hangmen. Easy to return the gold
of your vision to heaven, the rose-crown to the sunset
and the leaves' blood when we're the ones

who carry Icarus' kingdom in our arms.

Réponses du berger

I

Si j'ai reçu promesse un jour d'un autre ciel
que celui qui vous coupe les bras, je l'ignore.

Comme vous je souffre la tempête et le froid
et la fatigue insomnieuse; le désert me traverse,

l'absence des visages, tous ces poings de pierre
et le martèlement des vivants dans le labyrinthe.
Oui, comme vous j'ai peur d'atteindre au bout
du couloir, comme un nageur touche le fond,

de connaître que tout ici fut vain, chute,
faux miracle, qui ne portait l'homme au-dessus
de lui-même, là où la ceinture des ombres
se détache du cœur et tombe

avec la nuit parmi les accessoires.

II

Si le jardin depuis la première heure est clos
avec ses routes, ses montagnes et ses villes,
et ses oiseaux, et toutes les mers, et les couleurs;
si nul en secouant ses branches n'ajoute une feuille

à l'arbre, une marche à l'escalier de sa vie
en bousculant son ombre au portillon, pourquoi
courir ainsi d'un bout à l'autre de soi-même
comme un troupeau affolé qui piétine son âme

The Shepherd Answers

I

If I was ever promised some other sky than this one
taking your breath away, I know nothing about it.
Like you, I endure storms, endure the cold
and insomniac exhaustion. The desert goes through me,

the absence of faces, all these fists of stone
and the hammering of those still alive in the labyrinth.
Yes, like you, I'm afraid to reach the end
of the corridor, like a swimmer touching bottom

to know that all was in vain here, fall,
false miracle, which didn't carry man above
himself, there where the belt of shadows
detaches itself from the heart and plummets

with night down among the other props.

II

If the garden has been shut since the first hour
with its paths, its mountains and its towns,
and its birds, and all the oceans, and the colors;
if no one, by shaking its branches, adds even a leaf

to the tree, a step to the stairway of his life
by shoving his shadow at the ticket barrier, why
dash like that from one side of yourself to the other
like a terrified flock trampling its own soul

ou la laisse par touffes accrochée aux barrières,
quand la lumière inépuisablement coule ici
sur toutes choses comme le sable entre les doigts
de qui sait perdre, immobile et sans voix,

tout l'or du monde pour un babil d'oiseau.

III

Si je règne, c'est sur un bâton de buis
sans pouvoir sur le loup ni la chevêche
ni sur la route à toute allure là-bas
qui tire la montagne vers la mer

et mon front vers la défaite du soleil.
Je n'ai rien à moi, je suis nu, et comme
un arbre grimpe au ciel, je prie que la terre
se renverse en un sursaut de honte

et de colère à la face des puissants;
que dans la nuit ruminante, un dieu
tonnant change tout en pluie, en pleurs;
qu'avant le jour le visage du monde

soit lavé, et l'âme de toute créature.

IV

Comme vous j'ai vu le jeune homme grimper
dans le soleil sur ses ailes de cire, vu
comme il y croyait, l'impudent, comme
il était sûr d'avoir gagné

or leaving tufts of it caught in the gateposts
when light flows inexhaustibly here on
everything like sand running between the fingers
of someone who, immobile and silent, knows how to lose

all the world's gold for a twitter of birdsong.

III

If I rule, it's with a boxwood rod
with no power over the wolf or the barn-owl
nor over the road going full speed down there
as it drags the mountain towards the sea

and my forehead towards the sun's defeat.
I own nothing, I am naked, and climbing like
a tree up the sky, I pray that the earth
will turn over in a burst of shame

and anger in the faces of the powerful;
that in the pondering night, a roaring
god will change everything to rain, to tears;
that before daybreak, the world's face

will be washed, and every living creature's soul.

IV

Like you I saw the young man climb
into the sun on his waxen wings, saw
how he believed in it, insolent, how
he was sure that he had defeated

sur la vieille sagesse et sur l'air et
sur le poids du corps, et comme son visage
riait aux anges alors que tout déjà
avait repris son cours dans l'indifférence

des vivants pour les vivants, le pêcheur
ses filets, la vigie la barre de l'horizon,
et la mort sous le boisseau des feuilles,
des larmes, des regrets éternels,

son trou dans la terre.

V

Tous nous savons cela: qu'un fruit tombe
quand le soleil l'a gonflé jusqu'à la lie
et que la terre n'en peut plus de tourner
autour comme un potier reprenant sans fin

son ouvrage, et la fatigue tout d'un coup
le surprend, la nuit encombre ses yeux
ou c'est la camarde qui frappe dans son dos
comme un voleur, et le pot ou l'assiette

soudain sur le sol éparpille cent étoiles,
cent étoiles dans l'atelier, qui relèvent
un instant toute chose de la tenèbre
et de l'oubli: Icare, la pomme, ce que

tous nous savons et refusons de voir.

the old wisdom and the air and
the body's weight and how his face
was ecstatic with laughter while everything already
had gone on its way, with the indifference

of the living for the living: the fisherman
for his nets, the crow's nest for the horizon line
and death beneath its bushel of leaves
of tears, of everlasting sorrows,

for its hole in the ground.

V

We know this, all of us, that a fruit drops
when the sun has swollen it down to the dregs
and the earth has had enough of turning
around it like a potter reshaping his work

over and over, and all at once fatigue
takes him by surprise, night weighs his eyes down
or it's the reaper who strikes him from behind
like a thief, and the vase or the plate

suddenly scatters a hundred stars on the ground
a hundred stars in the workshop, which for an instant
raise every object up from darkness and
oblivion: Icarus, the apple, everything

which we all know and still refuse to see.

Le mort

S'il brûle sous l'essaim doré des feuilles
dans le jour qui s'en va, le front du vaincu,

s'il brûle encore, ce n'est pas d'un ultime
sursaut d'orgueil (j'ai tenu la barre comme

personne, j'ai tenu tout seul jusqu'au bout)
ni d'avoir cru happer d'un coup la lumière

insaisissable entre ses yeux qui charbonnent
—et les mouches déjà fouillent la cendre

des pupilles—ce n'est pas que le sang
de l'automne inonde sa nuque et la couronne

ni qu'en ce dernier regard les pôles
se soient touchés, non, c'est simplement

qu'un rayon égaré, le dernier sourire du jour
ou le reflet d'une épée dans la bataille des dieux,

sur son visage de cire enfin rendu
se repose un moment et frissonne

comme la chair des roses au couchant.

The Dead Man

If it burns beneath the gilded swarm of leaves
in the departing day, if the vanquished one's

forehead still burns, it's not with a last
burst of pride (I held the helm

like no one ever has, I held out alone till the end)
nor from believing the elusive light

between his blackening eyes could be snatched up
—and flies are already rummaging in the ash

of his pupils—it's not that autumn's
blood drowns the nape of his neck and crowns it

nor that in his last gaze the poles
met, no, it's simply

that a stray beam, the last smile of the day
or the glint of a sword in the gods' battle

on his waxen face, at last delivered,
rests for a moment and shudders

like roses' flesh at sunset.

Envoi

Je me souviens comme l'enfant tirait sa mère
par le bras, à gauche à droite: un vrai petit
cheval de cirque, et comme elle

continuait sa marche, fière et sourde statue
dont la tête coupée dans un autre temps
avait roulé parmi les fruits, les légumes,

dans le panier accroché à sa main
avec les projets, les amours, les mille et une
nuits d'attente rangés sur l'étagère invisible

qu'elle comptait, recomptait des lèvres.
Et lui tirait et sa mère résistait, sachant bien
de quelle valeur sont les ailes

confectionnées dans l'ombre avec des bouts
de ficelle et des plumes d'édredon,
et de combien leur poids dépasse un espoir

d'homme dans la balance des vents,
elle qui, tant et tant de fois déjà,
derrière les persiennes de sa chambre,

enfanta Icare en criant.

Envoi

I remember how the child was tugging his mother
by the arm, from left to right, a real
little circus horse, and how she

continued walking, a proud, deaf statue
whose head, cut off in another era
had rolled amidst the fruits and vegetables

into the basket hooked over her arm
with the plans, the loves, the thousand and one
nights of waiting, stacked on an unseen shelf

that she counted over, barely moving her lips.
And he pulled and his mother resisted, knowing
very well what wings are worth

cobbled in the shade out of bits
of string and feathers from a comforter,
and by how much they outweigh a man's

hope on the winds' scales,
she who already, how many times over,
behind the drawn blinds of her bedroom

gave birth to Icarus, screaming.

A Note on the French Poems

The original versions of these poems appeared in the following books, all published by Éditions Gallimard:

Un Manteau de fortune (2001)
Blues à Charlestown
Ô Caravelles
Parenthèse noir
Variations sur une montée en tramway
Max Jacob
Yannis Ritsos
Poète en Groningue
À la mémoire de W. H. Auden
Lettre à Félicien Rops
Le relèvement d'Icare

Le Pêcheur d'eau (1995)
Chantier de l'élégie
Pain de coucou
Un Voile d'éther
Le Noyer d'hiver
L'Or Bleu
Les dernières pièces
Emmaüs
Quatre saisons pour Jude Stéfan

La vie promise (1991)
L'Attente
La montée au sonnet

Bibliography

POETRY

1983   *Le dormeur près du toit.* Cahiers du confluent.
       Solo d'ombres. Ipomée.

1987   *Le relèvement d'Icare*, with Yves Bergeret. La Louve.

1988   *Éloge pour une cuisine de province.* Champ Vallon.

1991   *Chemin des roses*, with Bernard Noël, illustrations by Colette
       Deblé. L'Apprentypograph.
       La vie promise. Éditions Gallimard.

1995   *Le pêcheur d'eau.* Éditions Gallimard.

2000   *Éloge pour une cuisine de province, suivi de La vie promise.*
       Éditions Gallimard; Poésie Gallimard paperback series.
       Tacatam Blues. Cadex éditions.

2001   *Croquer la pomme.* Le petit poète illustré.
       Un Manteau de fortune. Éditions Gallimard.
       Oiseaux. Éditions Gallimard.

2003   *Badin.* George Badin Éditeur.

2007   *Adieu aux lisières.* Éditions Gallimard.

PROSE

1991   *Mariana, Portugaise.* Le Temps qu'il fait.

1996   *Verlaine d'ardoise et de pluie.* Éditions Gallimard.

1997   *L'Ami du jars.* Théodore Balmoral.

1998 *Elle, par bonheur, et toujours nue.* Éditions Gallimard.

2000 *Partance et autres lieux, suivi de Nema problema.* Éditions Gallimard.

2001 *Un été autour du cou.* Éditions Gallimard.

2002 *D'exil comme en un long dimanche, Max Elskamp.* La Renaissance du livre.

2005 *Auden, ou l'œil de la baleine.* Éditions Gallimard.

2006 *Une enfance lingère.* Éditions Gallimard.

Index of Titles and First Lines

S'il brûle sous l'essaim doré des feuilles, 126

S'il tangue un peu par grands vents, ce deuxième, 4

Si peu de lumière sur ma table, si, 8

Si tu viens pour rester, dit-elle, ne parles pas, 22

Six months later than the wild geese and a, 15

So little light on my work-table, so, 9

Songer à partir, disait-il, et c'était encore, 94

"Square à musique," 12

Such impatience, and for what, if tomorrow, 87

The evening sun in summer calms the game, 69

The mountains, the houses, the trees, 93

They've sold the old piano made of grass, 3

"To Cavafy," 87

"To Georges Perros at the Piano," 89

To leave (all at once, those shrill concierge's, 13

Un jour, la nuit s'établira sur toutes choses, 84

"Variations sur une montée en tramway," 80

"Veil of Ether, The," 63

Verlaine au fond de *L'Idéal Bar*, s'il, 4

Verlaine ensconced in the Ideal Bar, 5

"Voile d'éther, Un," 62

"Voyageur oublié, Le," 86

"Waiting," 23

Whatever it cost to make the old peasant give in, 43

What matters is not possessing only, 95

"Winter Walnut-Tree, The," 63

"Yannis Ritsos," 92

"Yannis Ritsos," 93